CLIVE'S LOST TREASURE

CLIVE'S LOST TREASURE

GEOFFREY & DAVID ALLEN

Robin Garton

LONDON · MCMLXXVIII

First published 1978 by Robin Garton Ltd.
9 Lancashire Court, New Bond Street, London, W1
Tel. 01-493 2820

Clive's Lost Treasure © Geoffrey and David Allen 1978
ISBN 0 906030 07 2

Produced by
Richmond-Davies & Associates Ltd
London, WC2
and printed in England by
Gem Graphic Services, Didcot, Oxfordshire.

The authors wish to thank the following people for their assistance and encouragement in piecing together the history of the *Dodington:*

Dr K. N. Chaudhuri of the Department of History, School of Oriental and African Studies; Mr Tony Farrington, Director of the East India Office and his staff for their help in searching through records and the Clive papers on our behalf; Mr René Lion-Cachet for being a great sport in agreeing to allow the divers to use his company's facilities on the island; Mr Eric de Villiers for his legal assistance and Arthur Astbury for his editorial assistance.

Bibliography

Clive Proconsul of India by James P. Lawford. George Allen and Unwin, London.

The Doom of the Dodington by Professor Vernon S. Forbes, Department of Geography, Rhodes University, Grahamstown. *Outspan,* September 21, 1945.

The Wreck of the Doddington, 1755 preface by R. C. Temple reprinted from the Indian Antiquary Bombay printed at the Education Society's steam press 1902.

A voyage to the Cape of Good Hope, towards the Antarctic Polar Circle, and round the World; but chiefly into the Country of the Hottentots and Caffres, from the year 1772 to 1776. London, 1785, and recent reprints, including that edited by Professor V. S. Forbes, Van Riebeeck Society, Cape Town, 1975.

History of South Africa before 1795: The Cape Colony to 1795: The Koranas, Bantu and Portuguese in South Africa to 1800 being volume four of History of South Africa. Reproduced from the Star edition, C. Struik, Cape Town, 1964.

A journal of the proceedings of the Dodington East Indiaman from her sailing from the Downs till she was unfortunately wrecked on some rocks on the East Coast of Africa by William Webb, third mate.

Gert van Bengel, a tale of Woody Cape. Cape Monthly volume three, July 1860.

Original documents, letters, diaries and company papers among the Clive Papers and records of the East India Office, Blackfriars Road, London.

Ordnance records of the Tower of London armouries.

Records of Fort St George (India Office Library).

The true story of the Grosvenor East Indiaman by Percival R. Kirby, Professor Emeritus University of the Witwatersrand, Cape Town, Oxford University Press, London, New York, 1960.

Public despatches from Britain 1754-1755 and 1755-1756.

East Indiaman The East India Company's maritime service by Sir Evan Cotton, edited by Sir Charles Fawcett, London, Batchworth Press.

Log books and diving records of David Allen.

The Public Advertiser July 8 1757 from British Museum files.

Records of Fort St George Diary and Consultation Book Military Department 1756 Madras printed by the Superintendent Government Press 1913 School of Oriental African Studies London.

The Indian Antiquary volumes 28, 29, 30, 31, filed at the School of Oriental African Studies of London University.

History of the Royal Artillery Volume One by Major Duncan R.A. London, John Murray, 1874.

Chapter 1

In the English winter of 1755, Robert Clive, later Baron Clive of Plassey, turned his energies to planning a return to India where he had gone seventeen years earlier, a pauper in service, and whence he had returned wealthy and a national hero. His two year sojourn in England had been bitter-sweet: popular adulation and social idolatry were countered by an unpleasant wrangle over the Parliamentary seat which he gained and lost in a few brief months. Now he was prepared to undertake the greatest challenge of his short life. At the age of thirty he had been chosen to end once and for all French power in India, and to bring peace to the interminably festering relations between the Indian viceroys of the Deccan, the great plateau of southern India, and the Carnatic, the area between it and the south-east or Coromandel coast. He had been given a lieutenant-colonel's commission in the British army, presented with a diamond hilted sword by the Court of Directors of the British East India Company; and been promised the position of second-in-council in the Company's Madras council, which covered the Carnatic.

Clive first went to India in March 1743 when his father, Richard Clive, found him a job as a writer, or clerk, with the East India Company. The voyage was dogged by bad luck and the ship, the *Winchester,* took fourteen months to reach Madras after a lengthy stay in Brazil for repairs.

For a boy of seventeen who lost most of his clothes during the hazardous voyage from England and arrived at Madras in debt, it could not have been a heartening moment when first he clapped eyes on that city, the principal east coast trading port of the East India Company. The town was dirty, cramped and dangerous. The British were crowded together in their own quarters from which they dared not venture by night and from which by day there was little reason to go except on company business. His work, for which he was paid £5 a year, was repetitive and unrewarding, the climate sapped his health, and he found few opportunities for genuine relaxation. Loneliness, home sickness and the slenderness of his resources made him so miserable that after a few months he decided to commit suicide, and gave up the attempt only when he had twice put a pistol to his head and twice pulled the trigger to no effect. After examining the weapon and finding it properly loaded he put it to one side, deciding that it was evident from this intervention of providence that he was destined for something great.

During these months, however, events were taking place which were to thrust him for life into the spotlight of world attention. When France and England went to war in 1744 over the Austrian succession, the two countries' trading companies in India managed to retain a truce in the name of commerce, which, however uneasy, allowed both to continue going about their business. The French were based mainly in Pondicherry, to the south of Madras. The British had secured their main port at Madras by establishing Fort St George to the south of the city and on the side facing Pondicherry, whence an attack, if it came, might reasonably be expected. The British Governor, Nicholas Morse, therefore felt secure, particularly as he had good reason to believe that a squadron of British men of war was on its way, and that this would immeasurably strengthen his armed forces and deter a French surprise attack, He therefore turned down a suggestion by the French Governor General, Joseph François Dupleix, that they should formally agree not to engage in hostilities, partly suspecting that Dupleix intended to lull him into dropping his guard.

Dupleix then turned for assistance to the Nawab of Carnatic, Anwar-ud-Din, who wrote to Morse warning him in no circumstances to attack Pondicherry. Morse agreed, but said that he could not answer for Commodore Barnett and his squadron as they were under the command of the King, and not the East India Company. When Barnett arrived in 1745 he agreed to respect Morse's advice not to attack Pondicherry as he had planned. Both men were therefore taken by surprise when Dupleix launched a small force against Fort St David, an English trading post sixteen miles south of Pondicherry near Cuddalore. The attack was postponed when Barnett's ships appeared off the coast. Dupleix retired to Pondicherry, incensed because Barnett and Morse, who were prepared to respect the Nawab's wishes ashore, saw no reason why they should not pick off French merchant ships with their valuable cargoes. He appealed for help to the French Governor in Mauritius, François Mahé de la Bourdonnais, who arrived off Pondicherry with one man of war, a rag-tag fleet of nine hastily armed ships, and a considerable army of men. By early September 1746 he and Dupleix had captured Madras, the very heart of British power in the province, and had begun negotiations for a settlement with Morse.

Clive, taken prisoner by La Bourdonnais, and his now close friend Edmund Maskelyne donned Indian attire and fled to Fort St David. Then in December Clive went as a volunteer with a small British force to mount an attack on Pondicherry supported by the army and cavalry of the Nawab Anwar-ud-Din. The action was feeble and neither side could claim a victory. The British force retired to Fort St David, where on March 16, 1747, Clive accepted a commission in the 2nd Company of Foot Soldiers at Fort St David. Soon after Maskelyne also accepted a commission.

During the next six years Clive fought a series of actions across the Carnatic against Dupleix. Sometimes he was supported by the Indian rulers; sometimes he was opposed by them – for they frequently sold their allegiance to the side they believed most likely to win; and sometimes the ostensible reason for the battles was to prevent them fighting among themselves. While the war could hardly be said to have been won or lost by either side, the result was that Clive's military prowess, his genius for rallying his inferior forces in the face of apparently overwhelming odds, and his stature among his enemies grew with equal certainty and rapidity. In the end, Dupleix was recalled to France to die there in penury, while Clive had brought peace of a sort to the Carnatic.

In October 1752 Clive sought permission to return to England, where the directors of the Company were already toasting him as "General Clive". The application was however delayed because the Company council in Madras felt the military situation was still unsettled. Clive argued that he was desperately ill, taking opium to relieve the pain of his fevers, and that he would not recover from malaria unless he had a change of climate. While the council reconsidered, Clive recovered sufficiently by February 1753 to marry Peggy Maskelyne, the sister of his close friend. Peggy had arrived in India only recently, but a strange link had been forged between her and Clive by Edmund, who wrote to her, and spoke of her to Clive, as if he intended an arranged marriage.

On March 23 Clive and his wife sailed for England together with another friend, Robert Orme. They arrived on October 14, Clive with almost unimaginable wealth considering his humble beginnings as the son of an impecunious lawyer and small landowner. For he had left orders in India that £5,000 should be used to buy diamonds on his behalf, or be paid into the Company account so that he could draw the equivalent sum in England.

The unmanageable boy who had been packed off to India at the age of seventeen now found himself a social celebrity. He was the toast of London and the country rang to news of his exploits. He joined the Whig party of Lord Sandwich and became Member of Parliament for St Michael in Cornwall; but his victory soon turned sour when the Duke of Newcastle, who now headed the government, challenged the vote.

At the same time there was disturbing news from India. The Carnatic had once again become a battlefield and in the Deccan the Viceroy, Salabat Jang, was little more than an office boy to the French general, Charles Castelnau de Bussy. The Mahratta Confederacy of west and central India had also become incensed with both the Viceroy and the French. They asked the British East India Company for help.

In their offices in Leadenhall Street in the City of London, where Lloyd's of London now stands, the Court of Directors debated the issues and in the end decided that the opportunity was too good to miss: they could rout the Viceroy and the French simultaneously. They asked Clive's advice; and he concurred.

Then came an offer from the Court for Clive to command an expedition mounted from Bombay, which would have the support of a British squadron of warships under the command of Vice-Admiral Charles Watson, recently arrived in Bombay to curb the wholesale piracy against British merchantmen on the Indian coast. Clive was keen to accept the challenge, but a problem of rank arose. The East India Company had since its inception retained its own army in India, but the government in Whitehall displayed little interest in that country. Consequently there was perpetual confusion in the chain of command, as evidenced by Governor Morse's inability to give guarantees of peace on behalf of Commodore Barnett.

Now the situation would be even more complex; for Clive, who would have to work in closest liaison with the 39th Foot Regiment which had recently been posted to Madras, was also to undertake a major military expedition with a high ranking naval officer over whom he had no authority.

The Directors of the East India Company, whose power in England was enormous (though not so great as that which gave them virtual rule over parts of India) were able to obtain for Clive a lieutenant-colonelcy in the army during his stay in India. The appointment was made on March 31 1755, and Clive immediately proceeded with arrangements to sail for India.

The prospects were magnificent. The directors proposed that once he had dealt with de Bussy and settled the problems of the Deccan, he should join the Company council in Madras with a view to becoming second-in-command on the retirement of the then Governor, Thomas Saunders. The council acted with the full authority of the Court of Directors whose decisions could take anything up to a year to be sent by sea to India. Its members were able to amass huge fortunes as it was the Company's principle that every employee, from the Governor to the under-writers, could indulge in what business or trading he wished once he had completed the Company's business. The opportunity to make a personal fortune was open to anyone: but for the councillors there were possibilities of wealth undreamed of.

In modern parlance it was an offer Clive could not afford to refuse, although it was to cause him some slight difficulty at home. The matter of his Parliamentary seat was still unsettled when his sponsor and mentor, Lord Sandwich, heard rumours of Clive's latest dealings with the Company. Understandably annoyed, for he had been lobbying on Clive's behalf, Sandwich wrote to him in March saying, "I heard for the first time last night that you was to have a Lieutenant-Colonel's commission which greatly surprised me as your seat in Parliament would therebye be vacated . . . If you would write me a letter in answer to this one to tell me you are determined not to vacate your seat, I might possibly retrieve some of the ground this report may have made me lose." It was typical of Clive that having decided to accept the Company offer he turned his back on the other prospects open to him as if they had not existed.

In April he his wife packed and prepared to sail.

While Clive and the Court of Directors deliberated over the political and military options, the Company's servants prepared a small fleet of ships to carry men and munitions to Bombay and Madras. To supplement their own Bombay-bound ships – *Edgecote, Houghton,* and *Pelham* – they chartered the *Stretham* from her managing owner, Captain John Hallett. From him they also chartered the *Dodington* for the run to Fort St George together with another charter ship, *Eastcourt,* and the Company ship *Duke of Dorset.* All ships were to carry munitions and food for the Company and for the King's troops and ships in India. The Madras ships were also to carry equipment for the red squadron which was lying off Madras under the command of Vice-Admiral Watson.

The *Dodington* also carried a company of Royal Artillery, one of four raised by the regiment in 1755 for service in India. The remaining three companies were quartered aboard the ships going to Bombay to reinforce the troops there during Clive's push against the French. The companies were raised and equipped within thirty days, and by the end of March were ready to embark. So hasty were the preparations that Major Chalmers, who was in command of the new companies, was ordered simply to promote the next senior man in the event of death or some other cause of vacancies in the senior ranks.

Captain-Lieutenant N. Jones was in command of the company which boarded the *Dodington*, though he was to hand over command once he arrived in India to Captain W. Hislop, who was already serving there attached to the 39th Foot Regiment commanded by Colonel Adlercron. Only three of the company aboard the *Dodington* survived the wrecking, and the moment her loss was known in England another company was raised at once to replace the men who were badly needed to bolster the dwindling company of men at Fort St George. The replacement company finally found its way to the Coromandel coast where Captain Hislop duly took command of them.

Company records and Clive's own correspondence show that the decision to allow Clive to go into the Deccan was taken late in January 1755. Clive had earlier tried unsuccessfully to book the large and dry round-house aboard the *Dodington* (a cabin or house on the after part of the quarter-deck). This showed that he intended going directly to Madras, and presumably to nearby Fort St David. However by January 31 it was decided that he should go to Bombay aboard the *Stretham:* the Secret Committee of the Company had already compiled its orders for Clive and the relevant authorities in India.

A large slice of Clive's fortune was, however, aboard the *Dodington*. He had consigned to her a chest of gold marked *R. C. No I qt* which according to the records of the Company contained 653 ounces and six pennyweights of gold. The records also show that the chest was put aboard the ship for "Robert Clive Esqr, governor for Fort St David". According to Clive's later correspondence the chest was worth £3,000, for after the *Dodington* was wrecked he wrote to his father a letter dated October 5 1756:

"Honoured Sir, the expedition to Bengal which I am upon the point of undertaking will not allow me to write a long letter. I hope to write to you fully and to your satisfaction by the next conveyance.

"I have desired by attorneys to pay you the interest arising from all my monies in England and the Bishop of Clintfort's (Clonfert?) annuity which is all in my power at present having lost near £3,000 on the *Dodington* and I fear a greater sum at Bengal ..."

These matters were however far in the future as the fleet prepared for the passage to India.

There is every indication that the *Dodington* was owned either by John Debonnaire, the elder, who died in 1756, or by his cousin John Debonnaire the younger (1724-1795) or by both in partnership. Both were wealthy brewers and merchants doing considerable business in Britain and India. Sir Richard Carnac Temple, a descendant of the Debonnaire family, notes in a footnote to his articles in the *Indian Antiquary* that he came across the original manuscript of the survivor's story among the Debonnaire papers. Until 1901 these were in the possession of a relative of his and of the Debonnaires, Major Charles Tennant, of St Anne's Manor, Sutton Bonnington, near Loughborough. Sir Richard also mentions that at St Anne's Manor he found the log book of the East Indiaman *Wake* and indications that the Debonnaires owned at least one other ship, the *Grantham*. Recently Sir Charles Buchanan and his son Hugh, who now live at the manor and are related to the Tennants and Debonnaires, kindly undertook to look for the manuscript on our behalf; but while they found the log of the *Wake,* they were unable to find the *Dodington* account. However it seems clear enough that the Debonnaires had a financial stake in the ship whether as whole or part owners.

East India Company records show only that Captain Hallett was her managing owner, which usually meant that in exchange for a share in the profits from the ship's trading, and a wage, he would undertake the task of running her. All that is known from the East India Company records is that she had previously been chartered for a voyage to India on May 10 1748, and that six years later she returned to Britain from Bombay and Mocha on May 25 1754.

Although the *Dodington* was registered as of 499 tons her exact size is unknown, and for a curious reason. The Company habitually cheated when recording tonnages because under the original charter given by King William III in 1698, all ships over 500 tons were required to carry a chaplain. This rule was continued under the 1702 charter given by Queen Anne; and *Hardy's Register* shows that between 1708 and 1747 all the Company's ships were with one exception under 500 tons. How much the Company saved by this extraordinary duplicity is unknown, but the practice continued well into the eighteenth century. There can be no actual estimate of the *Dodington's* size, though it seems unlikely that she would have been greater than 800 tons.

Though they are verbose, the Company's letters to the President and Council at Fort St George regarding the chartering of the *Dodington* and the cargoes to be sent to India give a fascinating insight into the shipping practices of the time and are worth quoting at length. Spelling, both archaic and plain incorrect, punctuation, and use or non-use of capitals are as in the original, both here and in the official and unofficial accounts of the loss of the *Dodington* which are quoted later.

The first letter was written on January 31 1755. In paragraph five, which was headed First of Shipping, the Directors wrote: "Since the date of our last Letter to you We have been under the necessity of taking up another Ship Viz. the Dodington James Samson Commander to accommodate the Government with a Conveyance for Stores, Provisions and Necessarys for the Service of his Majestys Squadron and Land Forces now in India; she is lett for four hundred and ninety nine Tons and is to mount twenty six Guns and is to be navigated by seventy Europeans including the Commander, Officers and Seamen, We have hired her for the Run from England to the East Indies and not to return to Europe again, which We have done purposely to avoid adding to the Burthen of shipping already on Our hands in India, after the said Ships Arrival in the East Indies and having deliver'd the Governments Stores and the Companys Effects and Passengers she is to be at the entire disposal of the Owners upon condition that she shall not be sold to the French or any other European Nation and that at Whatever Settlement she shall happen to be disposed of, the Governor and Council are to take security of the Person or Persons who purchase her, that they will agree to the said Condition. We are to pay the Owners for her Hire the sum of three thousand five hundred pounds Viz One Moiety [half] in England, one fourth part on her departure from Fort St George and the remaining fourth part on the final delivery of her consignments in Bengal. We are likewise to pay here Eight pounds a Head for every soldier and passenger; if she is detained at her consigned Ports for the delivery of her Cargo more than thirty days in the whole We are to pay after the Rate of Eight pounds seven shillings and eight pence a day for the time of such detention, this is a summary account of Our Agreement with the Owners which is intended for your immediate Information what further shall be necessary together with the Charterparty and other useful Papers will be sent you on the Ship itself."

Paragraph six details the Company's intentions for the ship: "It was Our first intention that the said Ship should carry all the stores, Provisions and necessarys for the use as well of his Majesty's Squadron as the Land Forces but the Lords Commissioners of the Admirality having intimated that there will be a want of Beef and Pork before she will probably arrive in India We have permitted the shipping a Quantity on the Eastcourt and Duke of Dorsett amounting to about sixty Tons on each Ship, this has in some measure prevented Our sending the intended consignments for the Company on those Ships to Bengal what therefore they have not been able to take in will be forwarded thither by the Dodington."

By this time the Company had decided to sail the *Eastcourt* and *Duke of Dorset* ahead of the fleet. The letter continues: "We send on these Ships the Eastcourt and Duke about Two hundred Recruits for Our Forces and Fort William Presidency as likewise four Persons to succeed as vacancys shall happen there ...

"His Majesty having been graciously pleased to give directions to the Board of Ordnance to furnish the Company with the following Brass Ordnance Viz. Two twelve pounders and ten six pounders Cannon and four howitzers of five Inches and an half together with Iron work for

Carriage shot, shells and other Appurtenances, also a number of Carbines for the service of Our Artillery Companys. We now send and consign to you on the ships Eastcourt and Duke of Dorsett ten of the said six pounders with Iron Work to make the Carriages for them, two thousand six pounder shott and One hundred Carbines, for the particulars We refer you to the Invoices and Bills of Lading, the remainder We intend to send you by the Dodington . . ."

Clearly by now the military solution was becoming the firmer of the options in the minds of the Directors, for they gave the Secret Committee, which in 1755 had four members, discretion to conduct any correspondence or make treaties as necessary. Regrettably Secret Committee documents were regularly destroyed and none now remains. Even aboard ship, captains were ordered to keep the Secret Committee reports in the round-house where they would be dry and safe, and were forbidden to open the packets until they were well beyond the hostile French coast. In a letter to the President and Council of Fort St George, also dated January 31 1755, the Directors wrote, "It being necessary, in the present critical situation, that the Companys Naval and Military Affairs; and the Directions to be (given) for Treatys and alliances to be entered into with the Country Powers in India should be conducted with great secrecy, We have thought proper to . . . empower the Gentlemen of the Secret Committee to carry on the necessary correspondence . . . "

In a later letter the Directors wrote specifically about the *Dodington.* "In our last General Letter of the 31st of January we gave you Summary account of our Design in taking up the Dodington, and the Terms on which we Freighted her, we now transmit to you the Charterparty Agreement between the Company and the Owners to which therefore we refer you for further particulars and expect your punctual observance of. But we must inform you that We have paid to the Owners the sum of Seventeen hundred and fifty pounds, being One moiety of the Freight agreed for, and have or shall pay to them, likewise in England, the amount of the Passage money for Passengers and Soldiers, you will observe, if the said Ship shall be detained at Fort St George and Bengal, if ordered thither for delivering her cargo, more than thirty days in the whole at both Places we are to pay Demorage [[demurrage – an allowance paid for undue detention of a vessel in port]] you must therefore, in case she proceeds to Bengal, forward the Charterparty and other necessary Papers on her together with an account of what money you have paid to the Commander on account of the Owners, and other proper Informations for the adjusting and finishing their account, you are to do the same to Bombay if it shall happen that our Select Committee acquaints you it may be for the Interest of the Company to continue her in our service for a voyage to that Presidency, but wherever she proceeds to you must recommend, in the strongest Terms, to the respective President and Councils, the taking sufficient Security of the Purchaser or Purchasers of her in case of her being disposed of, that she shall not on any Account or pretence whatsoever return to England again, or be sold to the French or any other European Nation.

"The Dodington Carrys a large Quantity of Naval and Victualling Stores for the service of his Majesty's squadron as likewise cloathing and necessaries for his Majesty's Land Forces, all which you must take care are duly delivered to, and accounted for by the proper Officers, she also carrys about Two hundred Soldiers, part of whom consists of a Detachment from the Royal Regiment of Artillery, being One Company of about One hundred and seven Men Officers included, the remainder are Recruits for our Own Troop, Besides all which sundry Goods are laden on the Company's account for your Presidency, the particulars of which will appear by the accompanying Invoice and Bill of Loading; We have likewise sent on her sundry particulars for Bengal agreeable to an Invoice and Bill of Lading enclosed in the Packet directed to you, which, on her proceeding thither, must be carefully forwarded.

"Should the Dodington Proceed to Bombay as before mentioned you must take care to forward her cargo intended for Bengal by the first safe conveyances, and if you, or the Select Committee shall think it for the Interest of the Company to detain her for any particular purposes, or send her to any other Parts or Places than are mentioned in the Captain's Instructions on the Charterparty the Captain is to follow all such Orders as shall be given him accordingly, and you are to make or cause, to be made a reasonable allowance to the owners, as nearly adequate to the Detention or service performed as possible.

"You are immediately upon the arrival of the Dodington, to make a particular Enquiry as to the Treatment the said Detachment of his Majesty's Artillery met with, and give us a faithful account thereof, as we are determined to show a due Resentment of any ill usage of them, either from the Commander, Officers or others, and we expect that you will do the same.

"We have permitted the Owners of the Dodington to Ship to the value of Fifty Pounds in Trading Guns, Shot and Flints for the purchase of Refreshments at Madagascar in case of touching there, on condition of their not being used for that purpose that they be delivered to you at Prime cost, you are therefore to Demand the same of the Commander accordingly, if you find they are not disposed of as beforementioned . . .

"His Majesty having been most graciously pleased to order Detachment of Three Companies from his Royal Regiment of Artillery to embark on the Bombay Ships, and we having laden on them a large Train of Artillery, We have empowered the Committee of Secrecy to give directions to the Commanders of the said Ships, notwithstanding their consignment to Bombay, to proceed, if the said Committee thinks it necessary, directly to the Coast of Choromandel, [[Coromandel]] to land the Military and Artillery, and then prosecute their voyage for Bombay; The Orders given by the Committee in consequence hereof, are not to be opened by the Commanders until they get into the Lattitude of Six Degrees South . . .

"The Brass Ordnance Shipped on the Eastcourt and Duke of Dorset and now on the Dodington for Fort St George, consists in the whole of Two Twelve Pounders, Ten Six Pounders and Four Howitzers of Five Inches and an half with their appurtenances, and several other Military Stores, particularly mentioned in the said Ships Invoices, The train [sic] Shipped on the Bombay Ships consists of Twenty eight Brass Field Pieces, of which Four are Twelve Pounders and Twenty Four Six Pounders, also Four Howitzers of Five Inches and an half with their appurtenances, and other Stores, all which Artillery and Stores are the property of the Company, being purchased out of his Majesty's Stores . . .

"In consideration of the Eminent services Robert Clive Esqr. has rendered to the Company while in their Employ on the Coast of Choromandel, as well as the further advantages which we are satisfied will result from his being again engaged to serve the Company. We have reinstated him upon our List of Covenant Servants, and appointed him to be one of our Council upon the Fort St George Establishment in Rank next below George Pigot Esqr. and to take his succession accordingly, if Mr. Saunders has resigned the Government or when he does, in that case Mr. Pigot is to be Governour of Fort St. George, and Mr. Clive Second in Council and Deputy Governour of Fort St. David, and to succeed to the Government of Fort St. George upon the Death or absence of Mr. Pigot, He takes his passage on the Stretham, one of the Bombay Ships, for the reasons which will be communicated by the Secret Committee to the Select Committee at Fort St. George."

Apart from the general instructions that the *Dodington* and Secret Committee orders should be opened in an area of reasonable safety once the vessel was at sea, Captain Samson was also given strict instructions concerning the treatment of the soldiers he was to carry and the manner in which he was to conduct the voyage. The pertinent passages in the standard company charterparty agreement read: "Put your Ship in the best Posture of Defence Quarter your Men, and frequently excercise them at the Great Guns and with Small Arms to make them expert upon all necessary Occasion inserting in the Logg Book the times when they are exercised. Trust no Colours, and avoid Speaking to any Ship at Sea, and in general be constantly on your Guard.

"You are in the whole Course of your Voyage to have a Clear Ship and be in all respects ready for an immediate Engagement in case you should be attacked by Pirates, and you are to keep your Ship in the best Posture of Defence until you get safe to your last consigned Port . . .

"We have put on board the Gallons of Brandy for each Soldier, which must be duly distributed among them in proper quantities for their refreshment and support . . .

"A Detachment from His Majestys Royal Regiment of Artillery being to proceed to the East Indies in your Ship you [[are]] hereby Ordered to afford both the Officers and Private Men all suitable Accommodations, and observe such a Conduct towards them, that there may be no occasions given for discontent and as We have given it in Charge to our Servants abroad to make a particular Enquiry into your behaviour on this Head, you may be assured We shall highly resent any ill usage they may meet with on board your Ship."

So it was that the *Dodington* came to be chartered and prepared for the voyage to Fort St George, though even the preparations for the trip appear to have caused some difficulty. In a letter written to Captain Hallett on February 21 the victualling officers of the company, Mr N. Jenkins and Mr R. Burgoyne, said, "The flesh designed to be sent in the company's ship *Dodington* to the East Indies for the use of Admiral Watson's squadron having been alongside her a considerable time we desire you will please to order the same to be taken aboard her."

(A similar complaint was made a month later, on March 17, after the *Dodington* had moved down river with the *Pelham* and been anchored for eleven days at Gravesend with the other ships. On this occasion the Company Committee of Correspondence received the following complaint from the Navy Office: "The master of the navy vessel carrying the provisions to be laden aboard complained that the captain of the *Dodington* kept promising that the stores would be taken in from day to day and that this morning the chief mate said that he can't tell whether (if he takes in any of the said stores) he can take the whole." Unfortunately the record does not give a reason for Captain Samson's odd behaviour.)

The bustle at Gravesend can be imagined as the ships *Stretham*, *Dodington*, *Pelham*, *Edgecote* and *Houghton* were prepared for sea. A terse but descriptive record of the events remains in the form of the log book of Captain Charles Mason, commander of the *Stretham*. Two months before the *Dodington* arrived at Gravesend, he noted:

Thursday January 16, 1755 – took on 1,456 bars of iron.

Saturday February 1 – took on 43 cases of copper belonging to the Honourable Company.

Wednesday February 5 – sailed to Gravesend and joined *Houghton* and *Edgecote*.

Friday February 7 – put on board by a hoy 33 cases of 1,043 loose plates of copper on account of Company and took on 40 Company soldiers. [[A hoy is a small sailing barge used for carrying goods to ships which cannot come further inshore.]]

Saturday February 8 – Mr Holt's hoy brought 160 chests of copper on board.

Sunday February 9 – men busy stowing copper.

Wednesday February 19 – took on 26 grapnels and 11 anchors on account of Company.

Thursday March 6 – *Pelham* and *Dodington* join us.

Friday March 14 – took on more copper.

Saturday March 15 – Mr Holt's hoy brought on one royal howitzer and a piece of brass cannon, their carriages, 75 boxes, 220 shells, and 350 iron shot/12 pounder, 2,100 of six pounder, in all 2,755 parcels on account of the Honourable Company. Plus 40 whole and 20 half barrels of powder for the ship's use.

Sunday March 16 – Mr Higginson came on board and took away 68 of the company's soldiers and put them aboard the *Dodington*.

March 17 – took on 30 chests of treasure on behalf of the Honourable Company.

Thursday March 20 – Captain Hallett came on board to pay river pay [[to the crew for their time while working in the Thames]] and we began to unmoor.

Friday March 21 – received on board 110 soldiers and their officers on account of the Company. 7pm unmoored the ship and hove short on the other anchor.

Note. Where, as on this page, material appears in double brackets within a passage which is already quoted, that material has been inserted by the authors; where material appears within single brackets it has been inserted by those who first reproduced, and edited, the quoted passage.

Saturday March 22 – in company with *Houghton* and *Edgecote* came to in the Hoe. On board one of the Company's hoys came things belonging to Robert Clive Esq and men employed in stowing them away."

The *Stretham* had now moved to the Downs, the roadstead near Dover, and on Wednesday April 2, amid great pomp, Clive went aboard for the first time to inspect his quarters. Captain Mason seems to have been mis-informed of Clive's rank, for he noted: "PM salute Captain Clive with nine guns on coming aboard and nine going ashore. Saturday April 5 – At noon saluted Captain Clive and his lady with a nine gun salute at their coming on board. Sailed from Hence, his majesty's ship the *Penzance* to the southward."

Stretham remained at anchor until April 12 when she was joined by the *Dodington* and *Pelham* and the ships finally sailed from the Downs on April 22. Captain Mason logged the event: "Light winds with driving rain weighed anchor and sailed east north east with the *Pelham*, *Dodington*, *Houghton* and *Edgecote*."

Some small idea of the East India Company's investment in such an undertaking may be obtained by calculating the total value of the cargoes shown in the company records. It amounted to £170,589, of which £14,496, together with Clive's gold and 30,522 ounces of silver bullion, were aboard the Dodington. It is not surprising that the Company urged its captains to be constantly on the lookout against pirates and to keep a straight course to their destined port.

Chapter 2

The first part of the voyage is described in Captain Mason's log. Almost as soon as the fleet left the Strait of Dover the *Dodington* proved herself a superior sailing ship and was lost to sight by the rest for some days. On May 1 Captain Mason noted that the *Dodington* was visible only from the masthead of the *Stretham*. Among later entries are:

> May 21 – Arrived in St Jago Road in seven fathoms one quarter mile off shore at noon, and here found the *Houghton* and *Dodington*.
>
> May 24 – sent 20 of our hands to help with the *Dodington's* rigging. *Edgecote* arrived.
>
> May 26 – the commodore made the signal for sailing and we are getting ready everything for sea.
>
> May 27 – Fresh gales, at 7 weigh with the *Dodington, Houghton* and *Pelham*.

Once again the *Dodington* outstripped the squadron and is mentioned no more in Captain Mason's log. Two further points from the document are however worth noting, the first that the Secret Committee orders were opened on June 14 in the presence of the chief and second officer (a ritual doubtless repeated aboard the *Dodington*) and that on June 24 the Chief Mate lost his life. On the day before, Captain Mason had gone aboard the *Pelham* with Colonel Clive and his family to attend the wedding of Jennifer Hill and Captain Galliard; and it was on the next day, while he was heaving in the pinnace used to take the party to the wedding, that the Chief Mate Mr James Hunt was knocked overboard.

We must now jump forward to the shipwreck of the *Dodington* after which the saga assumes a sinister quality. Two detailed accounts of the shipwreck and subsequent events on the desolate Bird Island were kept by the new Chief Mate Evan Jones and the Third Mate William Webb. Their versions support each other; but when compared with a third account, kept by Jones in such secrecy that he had it about his person during the whole time the company was fighting to return to civilisation, they are seen to paint an extremely bland picture. The secret document, which was intended for the eyes of the Company Directors only, tells a very different story of intrigue, jealousy, near mutiny and piracy.

Matters are further confused by the existence of a pamphlet printed in Snow Hill, London, for L. How which bears no date, and appears to be a more literary version of Jones's account, with some extracts from Webb's diary. As if this were not bad enough, Sir Richard Temple notes in the periodical the *Indian Antiquary* (in which the pamplet and Jones's official and secret accounts are all reproduced) that the original document written by Jones had been altered when he found it among the Debonnaire papers. It appeared that remarks and observations embarrassing or unpleasant to the owners were deleted. But from all the documents there does emerge a coherent picture, which when allowance has been made for bias in various directions undoubtedly approximates to what occurred.

The simplest way to consider the various accounts is to look first at Jones's "official" version and then at the secret version. This is the beginning of the official version, which opens before the shipwreck took place.

"Aprill [April] 23d 1755 Sail'd out of the Down's in Company with the Pelham, Houghton, Stretham and Edgcote. In a Weeks Time got Clear of the Channel in which Time Found we had the Advantage of the [other] Ships in Sailing which I believe is [was] The Reason of Captn

---

Bird Island: showing the bird colonies and the site of one of the survivors' camps.

Sampsons not keeping Company. The Next day, After leaving the Channel, lost Sight of our 4 Consorts, and the Day Following Discover'd Severall [several] Large Ships, Lying too off Brest, which we was [were] Inform'd by His Majestys Ship Dunkirk, was Admiral Boscawens Fleet [Consisting] of Twelve Sail of the Line. We met with Nothing worth mentioning after, till the 14 of May When we Made the Island of [Lancerota] and the Next Day Sail'd Through Between the Islands of Teneriffe and Grand Canary And [on] the 20th in the Morning Saw a Sail Which Prov'd to be the Houghton. And Soon After Made the Island of Bonanisto. The Next Morning we Both got into Porto Bray Bay, and Found Riding there [the] Pelham and Stretham who had Arrived, about two Hours Before us. On the 26th the Edgcote Arrived and Anchor'd here. The Next day we Sail'd in Company with the Pelham Houghton And Stretham, Leaving the Edgcote in the Bay. We kept Company with the Other Ships a Day, Steering S B E ½ E Which Course the Captn thought too farr [Far] Easterly: Therefore Order'd [ours] South, by [which] Means Soon lost Sight of them and Saw them No More. We had a Very pleasant Passage of 7 Weeks from St Jago To the Making of the Cape Land, [and] On the 8th of July Took a Fresh Departure from Cape Lagullas, we Run to the E'ward in the Lattitude of 35° 30' and 36° 0'0 S. till I made [we had made by my Reackoning] 12° 45' E' Difference of Longitude and by [the] Med^m of Six Other Journals 12° 50' Longitude and 35° 0'0 S° Lattitude. This day at Noon, the Captn Order'd the Course to Be Alter'd from E' to E N E. Had Dirty Squally Weather with the Wind from S S W to S S E and a very Large Sea. We had at this Time two Reefs in The Fore Topsails and three in the Main, and all the Stay Sails Stow'd so that We Run about 6 or 7 Knotts an Hour. At Midnight had About 70 Miles on The Board."

By altering the course from east to east-north-east Captain Samson was committing a navigational error which was perpetuated from the time Dias first rounded the Cape of Good Hope until long after the loss of the *Dodington*. In effect he turned the ship on that dark and filthy night directly towards an island named by Dias, and marked on the first Portuguese Roteiro chart compiled by Manuel de Mesquita Perestrelo in 1576, as Chaos Island (now Bird Island) "so called because it is so flat that it cannot be seen farther off than two leagues". It is not surprising that there was no time to raise the alarm aboard the *Dodington* as she careered ahead, swept by wind and tide straight toward the jagged rocks and reefs of Chaos Island.

What Jones, who seems to have been the navigator, did not know was that every chart in use at that time showed the south-east African coast cutting away too rapidly to the north, so that he was in fact far closer to the shore than he could ever have realised. When the ship turned on to her new course at midday she had been committed to an irrevocable disaster course; and at midnight when Jones checked the log she had less than seven miles to run to her doom.

Set on that fateful course the *Dodington* bore ever closer to Bird Island and her end. The night was dark and stormy, the ship's main topsail was treble reefed and her fore topsail double reefed as the captain attempted to make her more manageable in that furious storm. Shortly before 12.45 pm on Thursday July 17, the forward lookout yelled above the wind, "Breakers ahead and to leeward!" The helmsman swung the wheel hoping to turn the ship before she struck whatever lay under the water ahead. Little did he expect to strike an island; in common with Mr Jones and the captain he believed the ship to be 90 leagues to seaward of the closest land.

A front page article based on an interview with Mr Jones appears in the *Public Advertiser* of June 8, 1757. It continues the story in the following words. "The Helm was immediately put a-lee; but before she came quite Head to Wind, she struck lightly and then stronger; at which Time the sea broke directly into her forward, stove the Boats, and washed a good many People overboard." The crew battled desperately to turn the ship even then and head her back out to sea. Though they assumed she must be badly damaged they could at least hope to keep her afloat until dawn, when the best possible place might be found to run her aground and perhaps

Anchors: above: Dave Wratten measures one of the *Dodington's* anchors which had been lying in a rock pool for two centuries.
below: David Allen moving past one of the *Dodington's* anchors underwater.

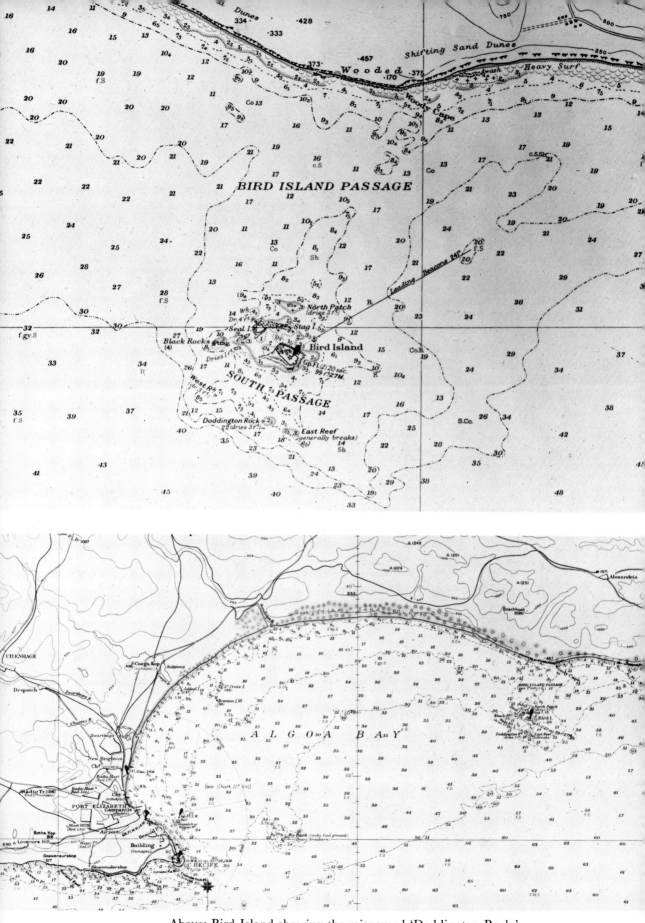

Above: Bird Island showing the misnamed 'Doddington Rock.'
Below: Algoa Bay. It will no be possible to disclose the actual site of the Dodington until the salvage has been completed.

even repairs could be carried out. But then, with the sea breaking over her she struck hard on a reef and the huge mainmast crashed down, to be followed by the other masts in a tangle of rigging and destruction. Yet still the sea was not done. Each wave lifted the ship and carried her farther over the tearing reefs, each holing her with a jolt felt by all on deck. Then she was thrown down on her starboard side and split open by a succession of giant waves, each of which took a piece of the ship's frame inshore with it until, as the *Advertiser*, has it, "The sea was covered with her Wreck". Finally the upper decks collapsed into what remained of the ship's shell.

Jones recorded in his diary, "A Quarter before one Thursday Morning the 17th of July The Ship Struck And in less than 20 Minutes was Entirely Wreck'd, Which is all the time any Body thought Themselves in Danger, Judging Our Selvs to be 80 Leagues of the Land; And When the Ship Was a Ground Could not See the Least Appearance of it Seing Nothing but Breakers all Round which did Not discover two Minutes Before The Ship Struck. Upon Which the Helm was Putt a Lee Immediately, but by the Time She Came Head to Wind, She was in the Midst of them [[the breakers]]. She went to peices in so little Time, that I am Certain Half the People had not Time to gett Upon Deck, for tho I got out of my Cabbin the First Stroke She Gave by the Time I Gott Upon Deck, it was Falling in And Other Parts Driving to peices faster Than any person Can Imagine." (In his account in the *Public Advertiser* Mr Jones said that while battling his way to the quarter deck the third mate, Mr John Collett, rushed below deck to find his wife and "brought her upon Deck in his Arms, but the Ship falling down at that Time on her Broadside, and the Decks falling in, he was separated from her, and never saw her afterwards . . ."

To continue Jones's private but "official" account, "Soon After I got on Deck, Spoke to the Captn and Asked him Where he Thought we Were, for I must Own the Main Land Never Enter'd into my Head [Thoughts] Nor the Captains [neither], for the Answer he Made me was, He was Sure it Must be Some Rock in the Sea Which Never was laid down, in any Draught [[chart]] for [I did] prick'd of that Day at Noon before he Alter'd [the] Course, as I did my Self After, and Found my Self by my Reckoning to the E'ward of all the East and West Land, 50 Leagues [and] dis^t from the Land abrest of us 100 Leagues Therefore Saw no Danger in Steering E N E which Course by the Draught Still Run us from the Land. I must not Omit Mentioning One thing More which the Captain Spoke to Me of Upon the quarter [[deck]] which was the only part Above Water, and the Sea Every Time it Came Carried Some away with it, that he was Sure, this Must be the Rock The Dolphin was Lost Upon and not once Spar'd to Tell there Fate, which Certainly Would be the Case with us and Indeed Every Sea Threatened it. [[The *Dolphin*, a ship of 370 tons, was bound for the Coromandel coast and the Bay of Bengal, when she was lost in 1747 or 1748. It was her second voyage.]] By this Time There Was not Above 30 People Left Upon the Quarter. He [[the captain]] Bid Me farewell and Said we Should meet in the Next World. Which Words Were Scarce out of his Mouth, When I was Wash'd off and believe Every Body Else, for I am of the Opinion Most that was Saved was Washed of by the Same Sea, for no less than 10 Mett in 3 or 4 Minutes time After they Came on Shore. Therefore was in Great Hopes Should have Seen the Captain As Soon as it was Day, But was Greatly Disappointed for he shar'd the Fate of 247 More, Only 23 Being Saved out of 270 and Most of them Very Much Bruised, my Self Escaping with A Few Scratches. As Fast as we Mett Gott Close together as we Could to keep us warm, for it Was Bitter Cold, and Nothing on but a Wett Shirt. We had not Seated our Selves long on the Sharp Rocks, before we Was Vissitted by Some Seals, which Was Taken by the people who first Saw them, to be Wild Beasts. As they Came Nearer to us Some said they saw 4 leggs; and Took them to be Hoggs, by their Making a Noise much like a Hogg. It was all this Time so Dark that you Could Scarcely See the Rocks we Satt upon, and now it was that I First Thought of the Main [[land]], thinking it Impossible for Wild Beasts to be On a Rock in the Sea, how Soever was Obliged to be Content'd with thinging so Till day Light when we Found Ourselves upon a Small Island, tho it Scarce Deserves the Name, distant from the Main Land about 2 Leagues Surrounded by Severall Rocks, Some of them two Miles in the Offing on Which the Ship Struck. Soon After day Light Call'd the people altogether, Found

Them to be The Following Persons.

Mr Evans Jones	Chief Mate
Mr Jno Collett	2d Ditto
Mr Wm Webb	3r D^o
Mr Small Powell	5th D^o
Mr Rich^d	Topping Carpenter
Jno Yates	Midshipman
Neal Bothwell	Quarter Mast^r
Nathl. Chisholme	D^o
Robt Beazly	Seaman
Jno King	D^o
Gilb^t Chain	D^o
Jer. More	D^o
Thos. Arnold	D^o
Henry Scance	D^o
Peter Rosenbery	D^o
Johanes Taylor	D^o
Jno M^x Dugall	D^o
Jno Glass	D^o
Dan^{ll} Ladoux	Capt Steward
Henry Sharp	Surgeons Servant
Leister	
Dysou	Matrosses [[gunner appren.]]
Smith	

There then follows further material which is headed in the original *Observations on Bird Island*.

"The First thing we did was to Seek Some Cloaths for we Were perishing with Cold and Several, so Bruis'd that they Could not Stirr. As Soon as we got things to Cover us, the Next thing was to look for Water which we Found in a Butt That drove from the Ship, and as we Were all very drowthy With the Salt Water we Swallow'd drank very hearty. We then went to work to gett a fire and As I had Often heard that Rubbing two peices of Sticks together will fire them Was going to try the Experiment, when one of the people Found a Barrell of powder with the Head out, Notwithstanding Some of it was dry. This gave Some Encouragement, to look for Utensills and Soon After Found a Small Escrutore [[portable writing desk]] with 2 Gun Flints and a File in it with Which we Soon kindled a fire This gave us all great Spirits and Indeed I thought the People would Never think they had Candles Enough, a light [a] Box of which was Found with the Escrutore. The people who Were most wounded got Round the Fire and the Rest of us Made A Tent Over them. By the Time this was Done it was Noon and Hunger Put us in Mind of Something to Eat. We gather'd up some pork that was Wash'd On the Rocks and Broiled Some Rashers for dinner. As Soon as dinner was Over I with those that was Able to Walk went upon the Wreck to See for Something to Subsist On. We Saw Several things Such as Flower, Beer, Wine, and Water but had not strength to get them up, so that all we Could do that Day, was to gett Some Canvass of which we made another Tent, not having Room Enough in the Other for us all. The Wind Southerly and Blows Very Hard And Threatens a Dirty Night and Indeed it proved so Bad that we Got little Rest being half Leg deep in the Tent all Night, it being rised upon Foulsdung I apprehend that on the Spring Tides and Strong Gales it Near Overflows [the Island]. I Shall add no More to this days Work then that I declare never Wrote a More disagreeable One.

"Friday 18 July. The Wind Easterly with Frequent Showers of Rain as Soon as it Was day

Light all those that were able to Stir went Upon the Wreck in Order to Save Water and what provisions we Could Find to last us the Time we Should Stay Here, which I thought Could not be less than a Month if those that were well Stay'd for them that was Sick; besides we all Agreed the longer We Stay'd there the Better it Would be for Travelling as the Summer Season Advanced. I went To the places Where I Saw the Beer and things Yesterday, but to my Great Disappointment found the Sea had Stov'd them all in the Night except a Cask of Beer Which we got up. But in looking About found a Small Cask of Flower, which we Also got up. We Lickwise Discover'd Some Butts of water, which we Endeavour'd to get up but Could not, for those who Escap'd favourable Are Still Very Weak, And the Cries of the poor souls, that is Hurt are the most Melancholly I Ever heard. While We Were Endeavouring to gett the Butt of Water up the Tide Flow'd and Put a Stop to our Work. The Day being far Spent went to Dinner on Some Salt pork as before. We had no Sooner Satt Down than Every body began to bewail his Ragg'd and Deplorable Condition most thinking they should Never be Able To Travel so far as the Cape of Good Hope or Delagoe [[Lourenço Marques]], which is the Only two Places there is any Hopes of Finding of Relief. Mr Collett was Consulting which Was the Best way to go, Saying he Thought the Cape the Nearest. I Answer'd I wish we Could find Some Tools, As the Carpenter was Saved might Build a Boat, and from that Time Nothing was Talk'd of but the Boat, Which gave New life to us all, and before we got up from dinner it was Agreed On; That a Boat was the Only thing that would preserve us from perishing. Upon Which Some Immediatly went in Search of Tools, and Others to mend the Tent better and it is with great Reluctance I end this days Work without Finding any Tooles except one of the ships Scrapers.

"Saturday 19th July. Wind W'erly and Fair Wea' Early this Morning: Musterd all the people I Could to gett up the Water and Succeeded So well that we got 4 Butts into Safety Before Dinner and Afterwards a Cask of Brandy and Another off Flower, with Severall Other Necessarys at the Same Time. Every Body was Very Diligent in Search of Tools but Found None. Notwithstanding do Not despair Being of Opinion the great Sea that was Continually Rowling in must Certainly Bring Some On Shore Out of the Great Number, in the Ship. Gott up our little Boat [w^ch] Was Always Stow'd upon the Poop on Board the Ship and Came on shore without being Stove. Lickwise Found a Firkin of Butter, and a Barrell of Powder. Some of the People that had taken a Walk Round the Island, Came to me upon The Wreck, with the most Pittifull Countenance ever I beheld, and Said the Side of the Island Next the Main was full as bad as this Side; therefore it was Impossible to [get] a Boat [off] without Staving her to peices. I must Own the Pittifull Manner they Told me this Peice of News Damp'd my Spirits at first but Recovering, told them Not to be Dishearten'd, that with Gods Assistance and Our Own Endeavours Should Overcome all Difficultys and as Soon as that I Went Round my Self, hope'd Should bring them Better News. After we got What Things We Were Able, Some of the People went And Gather'd Some Limpitts and Muscles of Which there is Great Plenty, tho not So good as in England. The Shell of the Muscle is Very Large and the Fish Vastly Small and Yellow. The Limpitts Are Very Large but so Tough, That we Could Scare Eat them. I Endeavoured To Perswade the people the Reason of their being Tough, was Owing to Roasting Them, and as Soon as we Found a Kettle to Boil them, Should Find Them Excelent Food.

"Sunday 20th July. Wind and Wea' as p' day past, had a Very Successfull Day. Sett Out Early in the Morning and no Sooner got on the Wreck than One of the People Found my Quadrant, and another Almost Whole and a Hamper with Several Sail Needles Files and Gimblets; also the Card of an Azimuth Compass. Soon After I Discover'd part of the Ships Transom – with a Chest of Treasure on it Mark^d and Number'd ... * Lickwise a Carpenters Chissell and Three Sword Blades. Another pickt up a Carpenters Adze and a Mariners Compass Rectified Which

* The chest was marked with a heart-shaped shield quartered with a cross and having the letter V in the top left-hand corner, and the letter E in the right, with the letter I in the bottom left-hand corner and the letter C in the right. According to Jones this mark was followed by the letters and number I A No. 5.

Gave the People Greater Spirits than Any thing Since we have been Here. About 10 o Clock we Went to Prayers to Return God Thanks for his Mercies, which as Soon as we had Done, went to dinner. All the Time We Were together our Discourse was About Building the Boat and the Difficulty of Launching her. Therefore as Soon as I had Dine'd and Sett the People to Work to get up a Butt of Water Mr Collett and My Self went to See if we Could Find a place To Launch our Intended Boat, as There is Nothing else can prevent us from Building One, having now got Some Tools, and make no doubt, Shall get Timber And Planks Enough of from the Wreck. It was not Long before we Found a Place, where there was Some probability of Getting the Boat of, tho it will Require Great Labour, to Clear it of the Rock Stones. We Walk'd round the Island Looking every Where but found no place so good as the First when We Returned the People had gott up a Butt of Water a Hogshead of Beer and One of Cyder and was at Work Making a Tent large Enough to Hold us all. I Told them of Our Success and the Illconveniancy that Attended it. They Were Greatly Rejoyce'd and Said they Should not Mind the Trouble. I Took a Turn With Some of the People upon the Wreck again, and Found a Smiths Bellows, Which we got up and Part of the Companys Packett tho almost Wash'd to Peices. However it was Taken Care of and put to dry, the First Opportunity."

The packets contained the company's secret and other orders for the captain as well as the documents and orders being sent to India.

"Monday July 21st. The Wind Westerly and pleasant Wea^r Sett [out] this Morning With great Spirits and before Dinner got up 5 Butts of water 2 Hogsheads of Brandy And One Cask of Vinegar which was all we Could Find at That Time; also Looked Every where for Tools, But Found None. The Carpenter Employ^d Making a Saw Out of a Sword Blade. Find the People Recover Surprizingly, Considering they Have Nothing to Apply to Their Wounds."

Once he had arrived safely at Fort St George, Jones told the Company he had also found a packet of Company papers on the day he found the treasure chest, and that he and Mr Collett had dried them out. Further he wrote in the abstract of his journal prepared for the President of the Council of Fort St George, George Pigot, that on the fourth day after the wreck he found a chest of wrought plate "which was no sooner got into safety than the People wanted to share it, together with the Treasure. All seemed to be resolved on it, excepting Mr Collett, Webb, Yeats and McDowell, which all refused, and from that time were used excessive ill, and at one time their resentment carryed them so farr that they proposed murdering us, and would certainly have done it, had John King gave his Consent; but his refusing put a Stop to their Villainous designs in that respects, tho' not in others ... "

"Tuesday July 22^d. Wind at S W blows very hard which Makes a Large Surf. Went upon the Wreck at Day Light in Search of Provisions for as Yet we have not Enough to Last us the Time, the Boat will be a Building. Found One Cask of Pork Another of water which we got up Immediatly. Afterwards Went to Work to Carry Plank and Timber to Build the Boat, Sails to Cover the Tent, and Cordage. I and Mr Collett Took a Turn Round the Island Again, and the Wind being to the Southward, Makes The Place we Pitched Upon Yesterday for Launching the Boat, the Lee part of the Island, therefore Much Smoother and Now Make no Doubt of Getting her Safe in a Calm Day. Upon Our Return Found the Carpenter had Finish'd the Saw, which Cuts Very Well the People are all Upon the Wreck looking for Water and provissions, Except Two Deans [[a footnote: Danes appears in the original publication]] one of Which Says he Served 2 Years of his Time to a Smith and Promises Great Things in Regard to Making of Tools. Therefore Sett Them to Work To Mend the Bellows. This Evening Discover'd a Smoke on the Main, Which Made Us of Some Thoughts of Going Over as Soon as Our little Boat is Repair'd. The People Returned from the Wreck without any Success than What's Mention'd."

There is a curious omission in Jones's account at this point – he fails to describe the burial of Mrs Collett, the wife of John Collett, although the event is described in detail in Webb's account. Webb tells how her body was found while the people were working on the wreck. They found "the Body of poor Mrs Collet, our second Mate's Wife, who happened to be at some Distance; Mr Jones, our first Mate, in order to conceal from him a Sight which he knew would most sensibly and perhaps fatally affect him, went to Mr Collet, and, under Pretence of Business, took him to the other Side of the Rock, whilst I, and the other Mate, with the Carpenter and three others, digged a Grave in the Birds Dung, and buried her, reading the Burial Service out of a French Common-Prayer Book that was drove on Shore from the Wreck. Some Days after we by degrees disclosed the Matter to Mr Collet, which, however he hardly could believe, till Mr Jones gave him her Wedding-Ring, taken off her Finger. After this, Mr Collet, who had ever a most tender Affection for his Wife, spent many Days in raising a Monument over her, by piling up the squarest Stones he could meet with, and throwing in the Birds Dung by way of Cement. On the Top he laid an Elm Plank, and thereon with a Chissel cut her Name, Age, and the Time of her Death, with some Account of the unhappy Catastrophe."

The grave and monument were found in 1814 by a British naval captain M. L. Fitzmaurice who incorrectly supposed the body to be that of the chief mate's wife.

Webb also records that the bodies of those who did not survive the wreck began coming ashore some eight days later; and each was suitably buried in the guano which covered the island.

On Thursday July 24, after the survivors had been on the island for a week, work started on the keel of the boat, which it was decided should be 30 feet long and 12 feet broad. Jones's account takes up the tale on Saturday July 26: " . . . . the Carpenters have most Finish'd The Keel, and Intend Making the Stern Next. Got up a Peice of 4 Inch Plank for the Purpose. The Smith Made himself 2 Hammers. People Employ'd bringing Up Wood for the Kiln to Make Charcoal. This Day we all Dine'd on Greens that Grows Upon the Uper part of the Rocks, the Leaf is Much like that of Merry gold; and There is Another Sort, which the People Bruise and Dress Their Wounds with, like Mash Mallows. We have 8 people Sick Now."

Jones refused to allow any work on Sunday and the whole company spent the day at leisure. The days of the following week proved not nearly so productive, with the survivors dejectedly carrying what they could find to the carpenter and with one unsuccessful attempt being made to launch the small ship's boat. Moreover the carpenter fell ill – or as Webb puts it, "The carpenter much out of order" – so that it was not until Saturday that any further useful work was done, and that only after the survivors had tried to provide fresh meat for themselves by eating a sea lion. This left five survivors extremely ill.

Throughout the next week little happened to disrupt the boat building and food gathering routine into which the survivors had fallen. The carpenter was again taken ill but recovered quickly; and Mr Jones notes that he "knocked down" some gannet for food but found the flesh very black and that they "eat very fishy." They were also obliged to go on short rations of two ounces of bread a day.

Then on August 4 the survivors were given a brief hope of rescue. Jones writes: "In the Evening, Mr Collett thought he Saw a Sail, and Call'd out with a Laudable [an audible] Voice, a Sail. I never was so Agreeably Surpriz'd in my Life, And all that was [were] in hearing Confess'd the Same, and Indeed their Behaviour Shew'd it by Running for Wood & Tarr to Make a Smoak, but upon looking With the Glass, Discovere'd it only to be a Spott [spot] on the Land that we had not Observe'd before. This Sudden Turn, had Such an Affect Upon the People that there was no Work done that day.

"Tuesday Augt 5. The Wind at N W & fair Wea^r The Carpenter Making Moulds For the Floor Timbers; Smith Making Gimblets & Trying Again at an Adze, which I am in great Hopes he will Finish; People Carrying Up Wood with Nails and Bolts in it, to Burn them Out, Lickwise Plank and Timber for the Boat. The Pork which Was Washed Upon the Rocks is all Expended. The Birds Which Were so Numerous at our first Coming on Shore, have Entirely left the Island, and the Seals Much Scarcer & Shyer, So that at present have Nothing to live on but an Animal Between Fish & Fowl. There is plenty of them Here and No ways Shy, they Walk As Upright as a Man, These Were Our Food this Day." The animals were of course penguins.

"Thursday 7th. The First part Wind N W Fresh Gales and Cloudy Wea^r with Some Rain, the Latter Hard Showers which put our Tent a Float. Got Another Sail Over it And Spread another

The Public Advertiser.

NUMB. 7056.

WEDNESDAY, JUNE 8, 1757.

An Account of the Loss of the Doddington Indiaman, taken from the Journal of Mr. Evan Jones, late Chief Mate of that Ship.

" May 27, 1755. Sailed from St. Jago with the Pelham, Houghton, and Stretham, and left the Edgecote riding there.

" 28. Finding that we sailed better than the other Ships, parted from them in the Night by steering a different Course, and had a pleasant Passage until we made Cape Le Gullas; from whence we took a fresh Departure the 6th of July. We run to the Eastward, in Lat. 35½ and 36 Degrees South, until the 16th of July, when by the Medium of six Journals, we made 12 Deg. 50 Min. East Longitude from Le Gullas.

" Being that Day, by Observation, in Lat 35 Deg. S. dirty squally Weather, the Wind from S.S.W. to S. S.E. with a large Sea, Capt. Samson ordered the Course to be altered from E. to E.N.E. We ran on that Course from 5 to 7 Knots per Hour, with Courses and treble-reefed Main Topsail, and double-reefed Fore Topsail; at Midnight had 70 Miles on the Board. About a Quarter before One in the Morning, the Ship struck, and in less than 20 Minutes was entirely wreck'd.

" It was a dark and stormy Night, and the only Warning we had of our Danger was calling out, ' Breakers a-head and to Leeward.'

" The Helm was immediately put a-lee; but before she came quite Head to Wind, she struck lightly, and then stronger; at which Time the Sea broke directly into her forward, stove the Boats, and washed a good many People overboard: Altho' we used our best Endeavours to get her about, it was to no Purpose, the Sea breaking all over her, and she struck so hard, that the Mainmast went away by the board, and the Rest of the Masts soon followed.—We could see no Land.

The Ship continued lifting and striking with every Sea, till unfortunately she at last laid down on her Starboard Side, and soon parted; every Sea driving some Part of her away.

" As the Larboard Side and Quarter was now the only Place above Water, all those who could, got there; she still kept driving towards the Breakers, and the Sea was covered with her Wreck. As Captain Samson sat with me on the Quarter, he said he had prick'd off that Day at Noon, and judged himself 90 Leagues from the Land, and imagined this to be some unknown Rock, where possibly the Dolphin was lost. We expected every Minute to be washed off by the Sea, and Captain Samson bid us all Farewell, and hoped we should meet again in the next World. Soon after we were all washed off, and in a little while, ten of us met on some ragged Rocks, and crept close together to keep ourselves warm.

The Severity of the Weather, and our melancholy Situation made us wish impatiently for the Day; but when the Light came it gave us very little Comfort, for we found ourselves on a barren Island or Rock, about two Leagues from the Main, which is laid down in the India Pilot in Lat. 33° 30. and called Chaos.

" By a good Observation with Hadley's Quadrant, it lies in 34 Deg. S. Lat. and Davis's Quadrant in 33 : 44. We were joined by some more who had been cast ashore, many of them miserably bruised against the Rocks. Of 270 Souls who were aboard, only 23 were saved, viz. Evan Jones, Chief Mate, John Collett 2d, William Webb 3d, Samuel Powell 5th, Richard Topping, Carpenter, John Yedts, Midshipman; Neil Bothwell, Nathaniel Christholm, Quarter-masters, eight Seamen, three Captain's Servants, one Surgeon's ditto, and three Matrosses.

" They remained seven Months on this miserable Place, subsisting on Fish and Eggs of Sea Fowls, with what Provisions they found drove ashore from the Wreck. During that Time the Carpenter built a large Boat, which they rigged like a Sloop, and called her the Happy Deliverance. While they were on the Island they made an Attempt to get Provisions from the Main, by going over there in a small Boat; but the Natives drove them away, and one Bothwell lost his Life on the Expedition. They found on the Island the Remains of two Wrecks; one seemed to be a Dutch Ship, the other an English; the latter least decayed, and by the Iron-work seemed to have been much less than the Doddington. It plainly appeared by Pieces of Glass, and other Things, that some unfortunate People had lived on that Place, and they could see the Remains of a Habitation, by the Stones being regularly laid one on another. They were very healthy while they were on the Island, notwithstanding the great Hardships and Fatigues they suffered, by Hunger and hard Labour. The 18th Day of February 1756, they compleated their Boat, and sailed for Delagoa, but were so long on their Passage, by Currents setting to the Southward, that it was two Months before they arrived at that Place. Unhappily there was a Chest of Treasure drove ashore from the Wreck, which the Officers wanted to preserve for the Proprietors, and the People to divide, which occasioned great Disputes, and was at last divided in Spite of the Officers. This, with a long Passage, and Scarcity of Provisions, made their Condition worse than when they were on the Island. A Biscuit sold for two Dollars, and every Man had only an Ounce and a Half of Salt Pork a Day.

" When they got to Delagoa, they found there the Rose Galley, Capt. Chandler, belonging to Bombay, who gave them a Passage to Madagascar, where they found the Carnarvon, Capt. Norton Hutchinson, bound to Madrass, who took them all on board. They sold the Sloop to Capt. Chandler for 500 Rupees, but she was seized at Bombay for the Proprietors. Mr. Powell came there in her; all the Rest went to Madrass in the Carnarvon, except Mr. Collett, Gilbert Chain, Henry Sharp, and Leicester a Matross, who died of Fevers on board the Rose Galley. Mr. Collett lost his Wife in the Ship; after she struck he went down and brought her upon Deck in his Arms, but the Ship falling down at that Time on her Broadside, and the Decks falling in, he was separated from her, and never saw her afterwards, until some Days after they were on the Island, when Mr. Jones and he saw her Body; but Mr. Collet did not know it, tho' Mr. Jones did, and had it buried without his Knowledge. Mr. Jones took all the Money and Effects from the People, when he got on board the Rose Galley, and secured them for the Proprietors."

to Save Water. The Smith Finished An Ax, and an Auger: and in the Room of a Better, the Carpenter Finish'd a Gun Truck for a Grindstone, which I hope will Answer the End, After we have Beat Some Sand and Shells, into The Wood. The Combmaker Finish'd the Saw, Which does but Badly, but the Carpenter Says he Can Mend her [it].

"Wednesday 13th. Wind N W & fair Wea'. The Carpenter Compleat'd all the Floor Timbers And began the Futtocks [[timbers forming the frame]]. The Smith Made Another Ax. The People Employ'd Clearing a Piece of One of the Bower [bow]] Anchor which Came on Shore on the Ship's Side. Got it up to Make an Anvill for The Smith, having One of the Steering Sail Boom Irons Before. Lickwise Found a Barrell [[Barrel] of Pitch, which was Very much Wanted, not Having any Before to Pay [[plug]] the Seams with.

"Sunday 17th. Fresh Gales E'erly and Fair Weather. This Morning Saw a Large Smoak to the E'ward on the Main Which Rises Our drooping Spirits a little, being in hopes it is Occasion'd from Burning their Land. Therefore Are in Greater hopes of Success, when our Boat Goes Over [[to the mainland]] which will be the First Calm Wea', After She is Finish'd. The Carpenter Intends going about her to Morrow. This Day as we dont Work on the Boat All hands is amongst [are Among] the Rocks a Fishing for [endeavouring to catch] Small Fish About the bigness of a Spratt [Sprat] We had the good Fortune to Catch a Few of, and this Week past has Help'd us Greatly."

During the week they took the damaged ship's boat which had been washed ashore to the launching place in the hope that it could be repaired and allow them to fish and make an expedition to the mainland. They also repaired their catamaran raft made with timber and rope, and built a second like it, also for fishing.

"Monday Aug' 18th ... The Smoak Continues Still to the Eastward, therefore Am Confirm'd it is Burning the Land.

"Tuesday 19th. The first part Fresh Gales Northerly the Middle Moderate, the Latter fresh Gales at S W; about 11 o Clock two men went out on the Cattamaran and returned in About 2 Hours and Caught 14 fine fish Which we was [were] Glad to See, being in Hopes We Shall not Starve As Our living was Very Bad Before; Wou'd not Miss Any Oppertunity to Catch Fish and Being Encouraged by our good Success, Mr Collett and another [Mr Yates] went out on the Cattamaran. Towards 4 o Clock, the Wind Freshned to the W'ward but they being to the Leeward of the Island and Finding the Water Continue Smooth did not Apprehend There Wou'd be any Danger of Getting in, therefore Continued Fishing till they Thought they had Caught Enough for 2 days in Case the Weather Should be bad And Not Able to go out [again]. They then Cut away the Stone which Rid them [[they were using a stone as an anchor]] because They would be better Able to put in without it, thinking the fish would make the Cattamaran Swim to deep. As it Blows [blew] fresh I was Apprehensive they Could Not get in, therefore Kept a Good look out when they Should Attempt it, Which I had not long done, before I perceiv'd they loos'd [lost] Ground, which Made me Very Uneasy. I Soon Alarm'd all the people, and the Only thing I Could think of to Save them from driving to Sea, and perishing, was, to perswade two of the People to Venture Out to them, on the Other Cattamaran, with Another Cable & Killock [[small anchor]]. Taking the Same for themselvs, and try to ride till it grew Moderate; And tho The danger was so great, that theire [there] was Very little probability of their Returning, two of them Attempted to go out, but was [were twice] Washed off Ropes Killocks And all. By this time, the Others were Drove a Great way. When I Found it was in Vain to try the Cattamaran any More, I got all the Cordage We had Saved, in hopes a Hogshead would Carry the End to them, but by the Time it was got Ready I Saw plainly it would be Needless to Attempt it, for they Were Almost out of Sight. So had quite given them Over, when [till] One of the men Came And told me, the Carpenter thought he Could make the Boat Swim, with One Man to Bail, [first] Stopping the Holes in her Bottom with Lead. And [At last] Three of the people Went out & Brought them in Safe, tho' with much difficulty, for them two [Messieurs Collet & Yates] Getting into the Boat from the Cattamaran, She Swam so deep & Leek'd so fast, it was As much as they Could do to keep her Above Water ...

"Wednesday Augt 20th. Saw a Smoak on the Main Opposite us.

"Friday 22^d. The First part Light Airs W^terly the Latter a Fresh Breeze, Southerly. At Day Light 3 Men Attempted to go out in the Boat a Fishing, but the great Surf on The Barr [Bar] Obliged them to put Back again. About 10 o Clock 2 Men Venture'd thro' it & Got to the Fishing Ground and Caught 30 Fish, but in Coming in, a Sea Broke into the Boat and Fill^d her So that the men as well as the Fish were Sett [set] A Swimming and with Much Difficulty got Safe on Shore on the Other Island About ½ a Mile from the One we Are one [upon]. A Shoal place from this to that Occasions the Barr [Bar]. At the first [On our first] Discovering this Accident, I was in pain for The Men, thinking they would not be Able to gett [get] on Shore, but Soon was Agreeably Deceiv^d, by Seeing them Crawling upon the Rocks. Our Next Care Was to Save the Boat, was in a Great panick about [which we were in great Pain for], but were Soon Relieved from that, by Sending the Large Cattamaran to Tow her in; and After [Afterwards] Fetched the men From the Island."

At this point in his narrative Jones has the heading *Transactions on Bird Island*, the first reference to the name the survivors gave to what had been called until then, Chaos Island. (On a "chart of the Eastern Oceans" printed in Britain in 1759 it appears as Confused Island. The name Bird Island seems to appear first in *Directions for sailing to and from the East Indies*, published in 1809, where it is recorded that a small rocky island "called Chaos or Bird Island is situated".)

Thursday August 28 saw the beginning of an adventure for some of the survivors, which not only provided them with an incredible tale to tell when they finally reached safety, but which to this day provides the backbone of the folk tale that a massive cache of treasure from the *Dodington* is buried on the mainland near what is now know as Woody Cape.

Jones noted on that day: "Fresh Breezes E^terly, this morning Mr Collett & 2 men Sett out for the Main in the Small Boat, but the day did not Turn out so good as it promised; for before they got one third of the Way Over, the Wind Freshened & looked Dirty, which Soon Made too Much Sea, for that little Babble of a Boat, So was [were] Obliged to Return. They had not landed ¼ of an hour Before the Barr Broke so Much that it would be [have been] Impossible for them to [have] Come in; however, Shall have the other Tryall the First Oppertunity.

"Wednesday 3^d. The first part Light Airs E^terly and hazey Wea^r. Latter wind W^terly. About 8 o Clock this Morning Neale Bothwell and 2 Others, Sett [set] Out for the Main in the Small [Jolly] Boat, & 4 Men on the Cattamaran a fishing. In About 2 hours the Cattamaran Came in, not liking the looks of the Wea^r and Brought in 3 Dog Fish & a Shark. An Ugly Accident happened to the Carpenter, by Cutting his Legg to the Bone and it was with much Difficulty Stopp'd the Blood. Kept a Fire in the Highest part of the Island all Night for a Signall to the Boat, but She is not Returned."

Chapter 3

In fact the boat did not return for three days, at the end of which Jones and the rest of the party were deeply worried that the men had perished and the boat been destroyed. But when it did return the men aboard had a remarkable tale to tell. Jones records it in his entry for Saturday September 6.

"Light Airs & Calm all Day. [Are] So am in great Hopes [therefore] of Seeing The Boat. At Noon Grew Very Uneasy at not Seeing of her, but Just as we Were going to Dinner, two of the people Came Running Over the Island, Calling out the Boat, the Boat, which I was greatly Rejoyced at, and Indeed Every Body Else. But [our Joy] it was Soon lessen'd: for Upon looking with the Glass, Could See but one man Rowing with Both Oars. [We] Therefore Conjectured immediately that the Other Two was [were] detained; but Soon After Saw Two [in the Boat] which Gave us Spirits Again, thinking the Other might not be well. So [we] Rest Myself Satisfied, till [She came] the Boat comes in, Which She did [was] in About an Hour after, With two only [2 of them] which was [were] Rosenburry & Taylor. As Soon as they Stept Out [they] of the Boat fell on their Knees to Thank God for their Deliverance [& safe Return to] this Island Again, Bad as it was. They Were Very Much Spent with Rowing And want of water & provissions. [We] Therefore helped them to the Tent & Gave them some Fish, which we dress'd Against [their Coming in] they come in, which They Eat Very hearty [heartily] & Went to Sleep. [We] Did not Care to Ask any Questions till they Awoke; when they Gave the Following Account. When th[e]y Were two-thirds of the way Over [they] let go their Killock and Each Took half a Cake & a draught of water; and then Rowed Again. About 3 o Clock got Round The point where I was in hopes, was a Harbour (the Land Appearing Double were) but it Proved no Such thing. [They] Row'd round Another but Still Found no Harbour. [Only] A Very Large Surf all along Shore. About 4 o Clock, they Pulld in Shore. Detrimin'd [Determining] to Land [which they did], but it proved Fatal to Bothwell: for as Soon as they got in the Surf the Boat Fill'd & he was Drown'd. The Other two, Just got on Shore with Life [their Lives]. The Boat was on Shore as Soon as they Were, but without their Provisions & [the] things they had for to Trade with. The first thing they Endeavoured to do was to get the Boat up from the Water Side in Order to Oversett her, & Sleep under her [that] Night; but being so tire'd [fatigued] with Rowing & Swiming was [were] not Able Stirr her [to do it]. By this time it was Dark. Therefore Took their Lodgings under a Tree, and by what they Told me After was [were] Surprizd they Were not Devour'd by the Wild Beasts. As Soon as it was Day light, they went to the Place Where they Left the Boat, but to their great Surprize Found She was Gone, but Walking a little way [farther] Upon the Sand they found her. She had been Taken off by the Surf & [was] washed on Shore Again. In looking round them they Saw a Man which they Walked towards. He no sooner perceived [them] than he ran into the Woods, which are [were] Very thick there. However, they went to the place Where they Saw the Man [him], & ther Found Part of Bothwells Body. This frightned them much, [especially] as They Saw the print of the feet of a Great Many Beasts. They then would have Gladly Return'd, without seeking [making] any Further Discovery, & Attempted to do it, but Blowing fresh and [having] a Large Sea Against them the Boat Over Sett a Second Time with them. Being Drove on Shore together [again they] hauld her up & as soon as they Gather'd a Little Grass to Eat, Over sett the Boat [her] in Order to Shelter them from The Wild Beasts. [In looking about] They found a Root as Big as a large Apple & not much Unlike a potatoe, Which Was Very Watry & [not so well] Tasted. However, they were Glad of that, Bad As it was, having Nothing Else to Subsist One [On]. They Saw Neither Man nor [or] Beast all this day; and at Night got under ye Boat, but did not Sleep much, for they Heard the Beasts Close to the Boat all [by them the whole] Night, which by the description, they give of them, must be [have been] Tygers. As Soon as they Perceivᵈ day Light, they haul'd Some of the Sand from Under the Boat's Gunnell to See if the Tygers were [still] About them for they had not heard them for Some Time before and tho they Saw None was [Nothing of them, were] Afraid to Venture out, till a while After. But upon Seeing a Mans Foot they Lifted the Boat & Gott out [got] from under. The man [soon ran] to two Others & a Boy at Some distance. At First they made a Sign for Our people to go away, which they Complyed With Immediately by going [endeavouring] to Launch the Boat, tho' it Blew Very hard at The Same Time. The Natives [they say then] Ran to our people [them] with their Launces in their hands & Rosenburry Imprudently took up a pistol (which Was Washed Out of the Boat when first Oversett, & found on the Sand Afterwards with the best [Boat's] Mast) and advanced towards them thinking to Frighten Them away, But was Mistaken; for they Spread themselvs and Immediatly Surrounded them Both Whetting their Lances, Rosenburry Ran into the Sea, and Taylor fell on his Knees & Beggd for Mercy. But they began beating him about the Back & Head With a Short Stick and Beat him till he Lay down for Dead. Then They pulld of His Shirt and Waistcoat and was [were] pulling of his Trousers, but being recovered from a Blow that Stun'd him, would not let them Take his Trousers, crying [making Signs] for Mercy. They at last desisted. Rosenburry Was all this Time in the Water. They now made Signs for Him to Come on Shore, which he Refused Signifying to them that they Would kill him; on Which they Pointed to Taylor as Much as to Say, They had not Kill'd him. He then Throwd [them] the pistol, [his] waiscoat & [sic] Trousers, and Every thing but his Shirt, and then Came to them. They did not Touch him, but Took the Boats Mast & pistol & Shew'd him how he Ran after them, & Laugh'd, Seemingly well pleased with Their Clothes, which they put on Immediately, Some [snatching] one thing & Some Another. They Took Every bit of Rope they found in the Boat. They Seemed very fond of the Iron Work & Took off the Pentle [[pintle, the pin on which the rudder turns]] of the Rudder, & was [were] going to Break the Stem of the Ring that was in it, but as Soon as Our People Perceivᵈ it [that] they Cry'd & fell on their Knees, Making Signs to them Not to do it; on Which they desisted. They then Made Signs to the Natives for Some what [thing] to Eat, on which they pointed their Lances to Our Peoples Breasts & Repeated the Same as Oft [Often] as they Ask'd. Rosenburry Took up Some Grass & Eat; Upon which, One of the Natives took up Some of the Roots, that lay by them, which I mentioned before, & Gave to Our People. When they found there was Nothing More to be got, they made Signs for Our people to go, but the Wind Blowing Strong, Wᵗerly, they made Signs that they Could not go. They then Made Signs for Our people to Cover themselves with the Boat and go to Sleep under her: and so left them. The Next Morning Proved fair Weather and a Light Breeze Eᵗerly. They Launched the Boat As Soon as it was Day. With Much Difficulty got through the Surf And row'd along Shore, till they Saw the Island and then pull'd for it. By their description, the Natives are Hottentots, Wearing a Skin like them [those] at The Cape of Good Hope & Clacking When they Speak like them ... "

Little did the survivors know how close they came to being rescued during this episode. For their own fires had long since been spotted by a farmer, Petrus Hendrik Ferreira, who owned land at the mouth of the Sunday's River, and it was his answering beacon fires that they had seen and which had rightly given them such hope. Had they made for the fires in the small boat the survivors would have been taken to the Cape overland in a short time and their ordeal would have been cut by almost three-quarters. Ferreira's concern did not end with lighting fires. He became even more concerned when he was out elephant hunting with another farmer, Andries du Pré, and met a party of Hottentots who told them they had encountered two white men on the beach who had come ashore from the island. Ferreira bought from them a pistol marked *Paris* as well as a blue cloth jacket, a piece of red cloth, a fine hat, sailcloth and woollen caps. Armed with these items, the story the Hottentots had told him, and his own knowledge of the fires, he reported the incident to the Landdrost (magistrate) at Swellendam, a Mr Horak, who ordered two farmers, Nicolaas Haarhof and Pieter van Vuuren, to make inquiries among the natives to discover whether the men were still trapped on the island. The pair managed to find the party of natives who had met the survivors, but for all they could factually establish the boat might have come from a passing ship. Dissatisfied with these results, and on the order of the Governor in Cape Town, Joachim van Plettenberg, Mr Horak ordered a well known hunter, Dirk Marx, to investigate. In December 1755, while the *Dodington* crew laboured on to complete their boat, Marx set off to discover what he could; but he too was only able to confirm the earlier stories.

The Swedish botanist, Anders Sparrman, referred to part of these events in his work *A voyage to the Cape of Good Hope towards the Antarctic Polar Circle, and round the World; but chiefly into the Country of the Hottentots and Caffres, from the year 1772 to 1776*, which was published in London in two volumes in 1785. There have been recent reprints including one edited by Professor V. S. Forbes of Rhodes University, Grahamstown. Sparrman wrote, "I remember to have read somewhere in an English Magazine an account of the *Doddington* ... On recollecting myself, and comparing this account with one I had from the colonists, it appears to me that this ship was wrecked right before the mouth of *Zondags-rivier* [[Sunday's River]]; as about twenty or thirty years ago, a smoke was seen proceeding from the island situated there. A farmer of the name of Vereira, who at that time was a hunting of elephants in this district, had bought of the Hottentots a pistol and a piece of red cloth, which they said they had got of some people who had come to them from sea."

Little suspecting how close they came to rescue, the survivors went about their daily labour with the carpenter busy as ever on the boat. On Tuesday September 9, after resting on Sunday and carrying out routine work on Monday, the party discovered what they suspected were signs of a previous shipwreck on the island. Jones wrote:

"Tuesday 9th. Hard Gales at S W. The Carpenter Employed as before, People Carrying round Plank and Making a Kiln for Warming the Plank for The Boats Bottom, on the Same place where Some Unhappy people had Made their Tent as we Suspected Some time ago, by Reason of A parsell of Stones being Gathered as I Imagine to Skreen their Covering from Blowing off. Their [sic] was Some Deal Boards Lay'd as a Platform under which we Found a Great deal of Iron Work, Such as Bolts Hooks & Nails, which Suppose was Burnt of the Wood, they made Theire Fire With. There is Some peices of Timber About the place Where we Are Building Our Boat, the thick end of a large Sparr and Some Railers & Boards There was Also Some Bolts, and Other Iron Work, found On the Other Island, but not so Much Decay'd as that Were the Tent Was One. Lickwise the Stanchin going down the Hatchway. with the Steps On it, which is Much Fresher than the Wood on this Island which Convinces me that Severall Ships has Shared the Same Fate of The Doddington, & I made no doubt but Captⁿ Sampsons Conjectures of the Dolphin was Very Just."

From this point the diaries of both Jones and Webb are cursory in the extreme, noting only the weather, the number of fish caught, and progress on the boat. On September 28 however an incident occurred which is played down in the public diaries, but was of major significance in the life of the tiny community. Jones noted on that day: "This Morning Found the Chest of Treasure Broke Open and above ½ Taken out and hid. Every body Denies doing of it, but Refuses taking an Oath Which Mr Collett Offered first." Webb was only slightly more illuminating in his entry, which reads: "This Day ... it was discovered that the Treasure Chest had been broke open, and two thirds of it taken out and concealed. Every Body denied knowing any thing of it. Mr Jones, Collet, and myself, consulted about a proper Method to bring it to Light and agreed to write down the Form of an Oath, and administer it separately to every one; Mr Jones begin first. But it was objected to by a great Majority; so the Matter rests for this Time."

Desultory entries on day to day food gathering and boat building continue in each diary. Both men seem to have become depressed, and uninterested in documenting the full activity of the group. In the case of Jones depression hits a low on Wednesday October 22 with the entry:

32

"Hard Gales Easterly and Hazey Wea^r. People Employed Knotting Yarns. This Day Try^d the Oven which does Extreemly [Extremely] well Making our Bread as Large Again With the Same Quantitys of Flower [Flour] Than the day we did before, which Was in a pan Over the Fire: but I am Sorry to Say it, there is not above a fortnight's More Flower at the Small [Flour even at our Small] Allowance besides What Allowance we Keep for Sea Store [Stock]; & I Fear have 3 Months More to Stay on this Island, before we are Ready to go away."

Jones does allow later that because of the huge numbers of eggs available they would not starve – on one day alone they gathered 800 after frightening the birds into the air. On New Year's Day 1756 he records that they collected 2,000 eggs and caught eight dozen small fish, while on January 17 two men caught 136 small fish and when they "raised the birds" they collected 1,800 eggs. He added that the company ate 400 eggs every day.

By now the survivors had become familiar with their surroundings and had named some of the rock promontories around the main island. One, about two miles west of the island, they called Shagg Rock (the shag is a type of cormorant); another, which provided the biggest supply of gulls' eggs, they called Egg Island. On Friday November 14 Jones records "About 5 Weeks ago I heard Some talk of Going to the Main, which I gave but Little Credit to; but all of a Sudden 3 Men took it in their heads, & Accordingly Sett off. About Noon they Returned Again, having been Close to the Shore, but did Not See any of the Inhabitants, Nor any thing Worth Mentioning. They Talk of going Again with the Cattamaran & Boat, the first favourable Opportunity."

They did not do so, even when they saw smoke near the shoreline on the mainland. But with the carpenter already so far advanced that he was working on the boat's gunwales, the survivors did start clearing rocks from the launching site and preparing sails for what was to be their sloop-rigged boat. They were also storing rain water in barrels and preparing against their departure in other ways. They still had two pigs which were to be slaughtered just before they left the island, and Jones makes an interesting comment on the animals' passion for birds' eggs. "Had Such plenty off Eggs for Some time past, that we afforded the two Hoggs [each] a Peice 50 p^r day. They Seem to like them so well that we are [were] Obliged to look well After them to keep them from Raising the Birds; tho' they Gett among them Sometimes & fill their Bellys before we [can] get them Away. And [They] would have paid Dearly [Dear] for it, Ere now, had we not Great Dependance on them for a [our] Sea Store.

"Indeed it is Not for what they Eat themselves but the prodigious Number of Gulls that give due Attendance And as Soon as any thing disturbs the Birds off their Nests, they Are Down as Quick as Thought and Devour the Eggs, but we Are Pretty Even with Them for they will have no Young this Year; for Their Eggs Being much the Best, Every Body looks Sharp for Them, tho' we Run a Great Risque of having our Eyes Pluckt out by them, so Inveterate are They Against us, that when we Are in Search of their Eggs they Come About us in Great Numbers & Fly Close down to you making a terrible Noisy Cry, & Sometimes Take their Own Eggs & fly of with them."

It is interesting to see how the men had become proficient in so short a time at doing for themselves and living off the land and sea. For example Jones wrote on January 13, "Moderate Breezes and fair Weather, 2 Men went a fishing and caught 4 Dozen Small fish. 5 Men went on the Cattamaran to Seal Island for Blubber. Carpenter Caulking, Baker getting his Flower [Flour] Ready for Baking; one Cask of Which proved Sower [Sour] Nevertheless we mix it: tho am Sure a well fed hogg in England Wou'd not Touch it."

After a period during which perfunctory entries such as "Moderate breezes and variable, with some showers of rain" and "Moderate breezes at south east and rain; got nine eggs from Egg Island" suggest some tedium on the island, Jones suddenly states without warning on Sunday February 15, that they intended to launch the boat the next day. The entry for what was to be the start of a major adventure reads: "Light Variable Breezes and fair Wea^r Carpenter Pay^d The Starboard Side. [We] and Got Ready for Launching to Morrow Morning. 3 Men went out a fishing & Caught 3 dozen."

The next day the boat was launched, a tribute to the skill of the carpenter and the endurance of the survivors who toiled so hard to make her. Jones wrote: "The first part a Light Breeze & fair Wea^r Latter a Fresh Gale. At 4 A M Began to Lay the ways for Launching, and at 1 o Clock Got the Boat in the Water and [gave her the Name of] The Happy Deliverance. Got The Mast in and Some of the Iron for Ballast and all Our Water.

"Tuesday 17. Moderate Breezes Westerly, People Employed getting their things into the Boat. At High Water, Haul^d out. When we Came to the Mouth of the Channel the Grapnail Came home, and She drove Upon the Rocks, which had like To have Demolish'd her, but Thanks to the Almighty we got off Again. Soon After Ran Over to the Barr and Came to an Anchor, to gett the Remainder of Our things on Board; and then Weigh^d and Stood to Sea, having on Board 2 Butts & 4 Hogsheads of Water, 3 Weeks Salt pork, & 6 lb of Bread p^r man, and 2 Live Hoggs."

Chapter 4

Jones's account of the voyage of *The Happy Deliverance* is so vivid that it is best given in his own words in a series of entries selected from his diary.

"Wednesday Feb^ry 18th 1756. The First part Light Airs, Westerly and Fair Weather, Middle and Latter Strong Gales and Cloudy Wea^r at 2 P M, Weigh^d and with Gods Permission, Intend to Make [the] River St Lucia Our First port: at 7 P M Bird Island Bore W B N. Distant 4 Leagues, the Extreems [Extremes] of the Land from N W to E B S. Distance off Shore 8 Miles.

"Thursday 19th. Strong Gales and Variable with Unsettled Wea^r and a Large Sea, Which we were Obliged to Keep Right before: at 5 A M it moderated [grew Moderate] which Gave us Some Relief, for while the Gale Lasted Every One Expected the Next Moment to be their Last . . .

"Friday 20th. Light Gales Westerly & fair Wea^r: At 6 P M Saw the Land the Extreems [Extremes] from N to N E Dist of 7 Leagues. At Sun Rise D^o from North to N W Dist off Shore 7 Leagues & at Noon from W N W to N E Dist 4 Leag^s A M. This Day 24 Miles to the S^oward of Acc^t which is Occasioned by a Current That I find by the Land Setts from N E. [[The mighty Aguthas current which sweeps down the coast from Lourenço Marques to south of Cape Recife in Algoa Bay. There are further references on March 1st, 2nd and 4th]]. This Morning the Gramposes was [were So Thick About us we Could Scarce Steer Clear of them, Running Right Over Some, but Drawing a Small Draught of water did not Touch any of them, But [tho'] Were Sufficiently Frightned.

"Sunday 22. Moderate Gales with Some Light Squalls and Hazey Wea^r. At 3 P M: Bore away to look at an Opening which Made like a River, but did not prove So. Haul^d our Wind and Tack^d Severall Times, in Order to try if there was less Current, In Shore than in the Offing, but Found it Sett us at the Rate of 2 Miles [Knots] pr Hour, To the Westward. At 1 D^o the Wind Came Fair Again, and we made the Best of it we Could; keeping about 4 Miles off Shore where we Found Less Current and a Cold Shore . . .

"Wednesday 25th. The First part fresh Gales and Fair Wea^r towards Middle And Latter Mostly Calm. From Yesterday Noon till 7 P M. Tacked Severall Times Standing off and On, but finding we Lost Ground, Came to an Anchor, And Began Immediatly to fish. And had Very great Success, by Catching Enough To last us Severall day's had we Salt to Cure them. We Are in hopes We Shall not want fish while it Continues fair Wea^r Enough to ride at an Anchor, Which will help out our Small Store of Provisions remaining; Having Expended Near Half already, and tho we have Run More than the Distance from the Island to St Lucia, by Dead Reckoning am Certain that we have not gott More than 30 Leagues on Our way. Try^d the Current and Found it Sett 2 Miles [Knotts] p^r Hour.

"Saturday 28th. Light Airs & Calms. At Sun Rise the Extreems [Extremes] of the Land from E B N to W B S Dist 2 Miles. Being Calm in the Morning got out Our Oars, and Row^d in for the Shore in Order to Anchor, and Land with the Small Boat, if We Could to Cutt Wood, having Only 2 Days Wood on Board. Anchor^d in 20 F^m Sandy Ground. Dist off Shore 1 Mile.

---

above: Stink Creek – the gully from which the *Dodington* survivors launched their sloop *Happy Deliverance*. The beguiling tranquillity is belied by the smell of rotting seaweed washed up by successive tides.
below: The *Etosha* in the quite average rollers by Bird Island. It can be gauged how difficult it was to bring salvage to the surface in such a surf line.

"Sunday Feb^ry 29th 1756. A Fresh Gale Easterly till 4 A M, When the Wind Shifted to the Westward and we Weigh^d at Noon. The Extreems [Extremes] of the Land from E B N to W N W Dist of Shore 5 Miles. I Never was getting an Anchor up with Better will than this Morning, for Yesterday we Lost One. Immediately let go Another which held us. Was in Danger of Foundering Every Minute. The Sea Breaking so prodigiously, and we Could not Afford to loose another Grapnail. Besides, in driving to the westward was Starving, therefore Could by No Means Agree to Slip, there being but Little Choice, Either to Founder at Anchor, or Drive to Leeward and Starve.

"Monday March 1st. The First Part Calm, The Middle and Latter Fresh Gales. At Noon got the Boat Out and 3 Men went a shore to Try if they Could Land And gett Some Wood. At the Same Time we got Our Oars Out on Board and Row^d. After them in Order to Anchor, but was Agreeably Disappointed by a Breeze Springing up from the W^tward, When we got within a mile of the Shore. [We] Lay too for Our Boat which Return^d on Board, without Wood not being Able to Land. Caught Fish Enough to Last us 2 Meales while we Lay too, And should have Caught Many More, had not the Sharks Taken away all Our Hooks, At Sun Rise The Extreems [Exremes] of the Land from East to W B S Dist of Shore 3 Miles. About 10 o Clock Came into a Great Ripling, Which Surprized us greatly [much] thinking it was Breakers, and for 2 Hours I Never Saw So Confused [a] Sea, Which Threatned our destruction every Moment. About 12 it Was More Regular which gave us Some Relief & as we Came Nearer the Land it was Quite Smooth.

"Tuesday 2d. The first part Fresh Gales and Squalls, Middle Calm, latter a fresh Breeze. At 5 P M Haul^d in for an Opening which Made Like a Harbour but did not prove So. As we Came Near the Land mett with a Large Confused Sea, Which is Occasioned By a Strong Current for When we Were Running 4 Knotts to ye Eastward as we Thought, We found we drove to the Westward by the Land at least a Mile [Knot] an hour. As soon as we discover^d Our Mistake haul^d off E S E in hope to run out of the Current but by my Observation find [found] it Continues [Continued]. [Therefore] For finding my Self 87 M^s To the S^oward, of Acc^t which made me propose [I propos'd] to the people to Stand to the S^oward, but they would not Agree to it, on any Terms, having no Wood on Board and Very Little Provissions. Two of them having [had now] no Bread, and Several Others Very Short. As [we had] have Now Nothing to Live on but an Ounce & half of Salt Port p^r Day, I propos'd putting Back to the Island to gett Wood, and Proceed for the Cape. Accordingly it was Agreed on & at Noon we Bore Away Lattitude Obs^d 33° : 03' S^0.

"Thursday 4th. The First part Moderate and Fair Wea^r but Soon Chang^d to a hard Gale and Dirty Wea^r With Very Large Sea. Soon After we got under weigh [Weigh^d] it Began to Freshen from the Westward. We Close Reef^d the Main Sail and got the Bowsprit in, then Lay too which was about 1 o Clock in Which Situation The Vessell Seem^d to Behave Well, Which gave me great Hopes of Proceeding to The Cape. But Soon After was Convinced to the Contrary; for When I little Expected it She Shipp^d a Sea, Which had like to have Wash'd all the Watch off Deck. Soon After that Another. So I found that we Should not be able to Cope with the Seas, We Were Liable to meet with in going to the Southward. [Therefore] I Propos'd going to the N^oward Again; which was Agreed to and at 2 Bore away To the Eastward again. From That Time till 9 o Clock, the Gale Continued to Increase and I think in all the Time I have been to Sea, Never Saw [any thing So] Frightful a sea as there was from 5 o Clock [till] to 9. For my part must Own I Expected to perish in it Every Moment.

"Saturday March 6th 1756. ... this day there was a Silver ½ pint Mugg Offerd for 6 Biscuits. Went to an allowance of Water 2 Qts p^r Man, having only 3 Hogsheads & ½ left, which will Last us About a Fortnight ...

"Sunday March 7th. Light Airs and Calms. Att 2 P M Got the Boat Out and 3 Men went in

---

David Allen at work underwater: working in the surf line visibility was seldom good. The yellow nets were used for lifting the salvage.

Shore to look for a Landing Place, but Could find None. At 3 Anchored and Caught fish Enough, to last us 2 Days ... At 2 A M. Weigh^d and Sailed Close along shore. Still meet a Current Setting to the W^{t}ward 1½ Mile [Knot] p^r hour. At 7 Falling Calm, Anch^d and Soon After Saw Severall of the Natives, Close down to the Water Side, At the Same Time Saw Several droves of Cattell [Cattle] Which Encouraged me to Send our Boat ashore Once More and try if they Could Land. When they came in Shore Found the Surf to Run [Ran] Very High, but being encouraged by the Natives who Seemd greatly Rejoyced at the Sight of our People, one Thos Arnold went on Shore, but had like to have to pay [paid] dear for it, Not being Able to Gett off Again thro' the Surf, but Sailing Along Shore 4 or 5 Miles, Came to a Small Bay Where there was a Little Surf by Which Means got him off and He gave the Following Description of the Natives at his first Landing. They Seem'd a little Shy of him, but he Advanced towards them Making Motions of Submission all the way he went. He Came to a Number of them Setting down, who Made Motions for him to Sett down, by them which he did. Then an Old Man, held up the Lap [Lappet] of the Garment which was a Bullocks Hide, expecting he would give him Something, and having a few Beads About his Neck, he gave Them to him. Then Another Held up his Garment in the Same Manner, And he Gave Him a small piece of Buntin Which was all he had, & they all Would be Glad to Accept, any Thing you would give them, but Never Offer'd To Take any thing by Force. Our Man made Motions to them for Some thing to Eat, & they gave him Some Indian Corn. He then went to gett Some Wood to Make a Cattamaran to gett of [with] on which they Assisted him, but he Could not gett her Thro' the Surf. They then Directed him to the Bay, Where he gott off & having Told the people in the Boat how Civill they Were to him and that we might gett Some Sheep & Wood if they would go A Shore again, they no Sooner Came on Board, but wanted to Return Which I did not Approve of [at that time], There being a fine Breeze Westerly, but those on Board, as well as [those] them in the Boat, Were desirious of Staying an Hour or two, Saying, if I did not, [they] would not go on Shore Again. Therefore, Consented, and 3 of them went on Shore Again, And Return^d with Wood Enough to Last us 3 or 4 Days Latt Obs^d 32° : 57′ S°.

"Monday 8. Light Airs and Fair Wea^r. At P M Made Sail [so] Close Along Shore, That we Could Talk with a Man: by Which Means kept out of The Current, Except when we Came off the Points Where it was so Strong, that it was with Difficulty we got Round them. A M, Saw Severall of the Natives, and many Droves of Cattle, Which they Seem^d to be very Carefull off, for when we Came near any of them that was [were] Feeding by the Water Side, their keeper would drive them to the Country.

"Wednesday 10th. ... As Soon as we Anchor^d we heard Severall People Hallowing to us, and Shew^d a White Flagg. We Could not go on Shore to them, the Surf Ran so High. At 3 A M Found Our Cable had Swept a Rock, Which Took us from that Time till 11 before We Clear^d it. Ran a Little Farther out into Better Ground. Sent the Boat to Try if they Could Land, but Could not ...

"Friday 12th. ... Cannot Catch any Fish here; Which we feel the Effects of, for those that have no Bread Are Almost Starv^d.

"Saturday 13. The First Part Strong Gales Easterly, Middle and latter Calm. This Morning 2 Men Went in Shore to Try to Catch Fish, but Return^d without Success, Assureing [Assuring] us there was Less Surf and in their Opinion might Land. Accordingly 4 Men went to try and 2 of them got on shore, and the Other Two Came on Board for fear it Should Freshen up to a Gale, as it has done [these] this 3 days past. The Two that Landed We Saw Walk along Shore till Mett by Some of the Natives, who Seem^d a Little Shy of them at first. We who were on Board soon lost Sight of them.

"Sunday 14th. Moderate Gales E^{t}erly and fair. Landed 2 More people who were Desirous of going a Shore, at the Time they Jump^d out of the Boat a Shark Took Hold of one of the Peoples Oars, and Almost pull^d it from him. Towards Night Less Wind and [looked] looks as if it would Shift to the Westward, Which Made me Very Uneasy for the People that Were on Shore; least [lest] it Should Blow so hard that Should not be Able to wait till Morning; so Made Signalls in the Night by Shewing Lights in hopes it Would Fetch Them down to the Water Side, when we might Have got them off; but it was to no purpose, for they did not Come down till 6 o Clock next Morning, when it was to [too] Late, There being a Gale of wind and to [too] much Sea for the Small Boat. So we Wav^d [as we sail'd] along Shore. After we had Run about 4 or 5 Miles Came to a Small Bay Where there was Shelter from a Westerly Wind. Anchor^d in 5 F^m Water 4 Men went on Shore. 2 to meet the 4 that [were] was left Behind & 2 to Sound at Y^e Mouth of a River Within us, Which [we] Are in great hopes Shall gett into in About 3 Hours. The 2 Men Return^d With the Other 4 and Severall of the Natives. We Are Expecting them on Board Every Minute, butt whether the Surf is to High or the Boat Stove Cannot Tell, for they do not Attempt to Come off.

"Monday March 15th 1756. The First Part a Fresh Gale Westerly with Squalls & hard Rain, Middle Calm, Latter a Light Air Easterly. Was Very Uneasy all Night, for The people and Boats. As Soon as it was Day light weigh^d & Stood Close in Shore to Call to Them, Threatning if they did not Come off would go away And Leave them; for While we Lay [Lie] here, Are Expending what Little provissions we have Left not Catching any Fish, and Very Little Expectation of Getting into the River [[Sir Richard Temple's footnote suggests either St Paul's Cove and the River St John, or alternatively the Umzimbuvu River in the Transkei]]; there being a very great Bar. Our Threatning had [its] the Desired Effect: for two of them Ventured off tho' there was a Great Surf on the Shore. The Reason they did not Come off before, Was on Account of the Surf. They Were Very well Used by the Natives, Who gave them Bread, Milk and Fruit: the Wind is Come Easterly which Makes the place We Are in a Bad road, & is a fair Wind into the River, Which with the Civil Usage of the Natives & Our people on Shore, Tempts us Very Much to Hazard going over the Barr, Which was Agreed On. At 10 o Clock Weigh^d and Run for the River, the Small Boat a head a Sounding [[measuring the depth with lead and line]]. They made a Signal for us to Haul of. Upon which we Wore and Anchor^d again. They Informed us [they] had but 8 Foot Water, Which we Thought to Little, with the Sand She would have. Therefore Agreed to Wait till High Water. At 2 in the Afternoon Weigh^d with a fresh Breeze E^terly, and run Over the Barr, Much Safer than we Expected, and Came to Anchor, in the River in ¼ less three Fathoms. At Spring Tides have 3 Fathom at high Water: & 8 Foot att Low Water; Mr Collet & my Self Went on Shore to get Provissions, & Bought a Fine Bullock ... for a pair of Copper Bangles for their [the Natives] Arms, and Some Small peices of Iron. We kill^d the Bullock Immediately and Supp^d very Heartily Upon it.

"Tuesday 16th. Wind Variable & fair Wea^r. This Morning there is but few of the Natives to be Seen. And [I don't find] They have Nothing for Our Use. In the Afternoon I went about 5 Miles up the River Taking on [one] of the Natives With me, by Whose Assistance I got about 2 Peck of Grain giving them Brass Buttons in return. [I] Saw a Great Number of Mannates or Sea Cows in the River. As Soon as I Returnd on Board, Sent the Boat, for [Those] them Who Were Opposite the Vessell a trading. They got Only as Much Bread As Would Serve A Meal. We have not been On Shore on the East Side, being much discouraged, by the people on the W^t Side, telling us they would Cutt our Throats.

In his diary Webb says that members of the crew wishing to barter would show what they wanted by "kneeling down and Gnawing the grass, and holding our Hands up like Horns, and making a Noise like that of Bullicks, Sheep, & c which they soon understood, and were very expeditious in driving down two small Bullocks, which we soon agreed for, and purchased for about one Pound of Copper and three or four Brass Buttons, each Bullock weighing about five or six Hundred ... They likewise brought down Milk in great Quantities, which we used to purchase at a very cheap Rate, giving only a Brass Button for about two or three Gallons. Likewise a small Grain like Guinea wheat, which we purchased at the same Rate, and ground it into two stones, and baked it upon some Embers for Bread, in Hopes it would keep till we could get better; but this did not succeed, for it grew mouldy in three Days, therefore we afterwards boiled it with our Meat and found it very good Food. We stayed here about a Fortnight, during which Time we often went up in the Country to their Towns about ten or twelve Miles, where they lived in Huts covered with Rushes like a kind of Thatch, which were very neat within, and they always offered one for us to lay in if we staid on shore all Night, and were extremely obliging. At these Times we used to eat with them, and they liked our way of dressing Victuals, though they are particularly fond of the Intrails, such as the Paunch and Guts, which they mostly eat raw, only shaking out the Excrement. They were pleased at coming on board our Boat, often went up the River in the small Boat with us, and behaved very sociably. They were no ways shy of their women, but frequently brought their own Sisters and Daughters and left them for a whole Day with us, when they were going into the woods which are very plenty hereabouts. Their chief Excercise is hunting, and their only Arms are Launces and two short sticks with a Knob at the End [[known in South Africa as knobkerries]] with which, having wounded their Game with the Launce, they knock it down.

"The River here is very full of Manattes or Seacows which we found no ways mischievous: They mostly come on Shore in the Night, and their chief Food is Grass; the Natives sometimes catch them asleep and kill them to eat. They have a few Elephants Teeth, which they offered very cheap, but we had no Room to stow them in our Boat. They wear little or no Cloathing in the Day-time, and in the Night only a Bullock's Hide, which they dry thoroughly and make them very supple. Their chief Ornaments are a Piece of a Bullock's Tail, which hangs dangling down from their Rump to their Heels, with a few small Sea Shells tied to it; they also wear small Pieces of the Skin tied round their Knees, Ankles and Arms. Their Hair they plaister up with a great Quantity of Tallow or Fat mixed with a kind of red Earth, and they rub their Bodies all over with Grease. They are prodigious active and dextrous with their Launces; we often saw them throw a Launce thirty or forty Yards, and hit a small Head of Corn. They have another Method of exercising themselves in the Day, and commonly when they meet or part from one another, and that is by dancing and jumping all round a Ring, and making a most hideous Noise, sometimes hallowing and sometimes grunting like a Hog; then running backwards and forwards as hard as they can, flourishing their Launces. Another Circumstance I forgot to remark, which perhaps may be a little surprising; which is, that among these Natives, who are entirely black and all wooly haired, we met with a Youth, seemingly about 12 or 14 Years of Age, quite white and his Features had the true Resemblance of an European, having fine light Hair, not in the least ressembling that of the other Natives. We further observed, that this Boy was made use of as a kind of Domestic; for they sent him on Errands and sometimes would not let him eat with them, but made him stay till they had done; tho I must do them the Justice to say I never saw a more amicable Sort of Folks among themselves than they are; for if they have any thing to eat, be it ever so little, the Person who has it divides it equally as far as it goes with a seeming Pleasure. For about two or three Days before our Departure the abovementioned Boy was not to be seen, they being under some Apprehensions of his going away with us, as we imagined; and the Morning we came away we could not see one of the Natives."

For the departure we return to Jones's narrative:

"Monday 29th. Wind Northerly and fair Wea[r]. At 5 A M Weigh[d] and Soon got to the Barr Where we Found More Surf than we Expected, and had it Been Day Light Enough for us to have Seen it, before we Came Near it, I am Certain Should not have Attempted Coming Over it; for When we Got Among the Breakers found them Allmost to many for us, 2 Very large Seas Braking Right on us, Another Hove the Boat Broadside to the Sea, but Luckily She wore [[turned round]] before Another Sea, took her, or Else must Inevitably been Lost on the Rocks, which [were] was Not Twice her Length from us. However, Got Safe out, & hope Shall not be Necessitated to put into a Barr Harbour Again."

The week passed with the sloop making slow progress along the coast until Monday April 5 when Jones sighted what he thought to be the River St Lucia, but which seems more likely to have been a river farther south. "At 9 P M Anchor[d] Near the Opening. Intended to go in [on] in the Morning if it proved So, Which it did, butt Appearing to be a Bar Harbour & the Wind Continuing Westerly [we] Made Sail. Sometime made an Opening Where we Saw no Surf. The Wind Tempts us to keep [On] One to the Eastward. At Noon the Wind Came To the Eastward

& We Bore away for the River St Lucia. At 3 P M anchor^d about 1 Mile from the Entrance which Broke Right a Cross, so that we did not Care for going in, tho' it did not Appear so Dangerous as the Other. In the Night it Blew Fresh, & We Rid Very hard, Latt^d Obs^d 28° : 16′ S°.

"Tuesday 6. This Morning Little Wind. Tho' it Blew fresh all Night East^{r}ly (Which is Right in the Harbour) there was butt Little Surf, Therefore, it was Agreed on to go in. Accordingly Weigh and Gott Safe Over having No less than 10 Foot Water. In Running up the River to Anchor, Grounded Upon a Sand, but Recov^d the Damage, and got her off Again Next Side. And [We then] Moor^d in 3 Fathom Water. While we Lay a Ground, the Natives Came on Each Side of the River. We Sent on Shore to Them, and by motions Soon Made them Understand we wanted Some Bullocks, Which they Immediatly Brought, but for want of Brass Toys, Could not Buy any. Gott about 4 dozen of Fowls for Brass Buttons."

Once again it is Webb who made the more interesting and detailed notes of this encounter which lasted twelve days. He wrote: " . . . we spent most of our Time in walking about the Country, and seeing their Towns and Method of living, and endeavoured to carry on a pretty Trade for what we wanted. They seeming to have a great Veneration for Brass, we carried a Brass Handle of an old Chest with us, and showed it them, for which they immediately offered us two Bullocks, which we readily agreed to; and they drove them down to our Boat. We found there a haughty, proud sort of People, and not altogether so honest as the former, having detected the principal Governor, who we had already paid for a Lodging in one of their Huts for the Night, stealing some Pieces of Iron we had with us in a Basket, to defray our Expences till our Return to the Boat. [[Having reached Natal the party were almost certainly dealing with Zulus, whose reputation as a proud and defiant race is legendary.]] We staid two or three Days with them in the Country, in which Time we never could get them to eat with us, nor would they let us eat with them. They likewise differed greatly from the other People aforementioned in their Cookery, as they dress all their Victuals in a very cleanly Manner, and are likewise very cleanly in their Bodies; for the first Thing they do in the Morning is to wash themselves all over; then they go to some Kind of Devotion, which we never observed in the others. Neither have these any of the same Ornaments as the others use. They pride themselves much in their Hair, which they dress up very neatly; and they are extremely shy in regard to their Women. Their Arms are the same as the others, and also their Diversions. We found a few Men here who came from *Delagoa*, and had some Ambergrease and Elephant's Teeth to dispose of. The latter in great plenty.

"Sunday 18. A pleasant Gale westerly; and fair weather. At seven in the Morning being all on board, weighed and made sail; about a Quarter before High-water, when we were got almost to the Bar, our People very imprudently hauled the Sails down and let go the Grapnail close to the brake of a Sand, and nine of them got the Boat out and went on Shore, swearing bitterly that they would sooner take their chance of living among the Natives than be drowned in attempting to go over the Bar; so the rest of us who remained on board, were either to venture over the bar, or to go on Shore, the Vessel not being able to get back, the wind and tide setting both out of the River, so that before half ebb the would ground and bent to Pieces. Therefore, in Hopes to save ourselves and the boat, we weighed in God's name, and soon got to the breakers; there we lay beating in a dismal condition, having no more than eight foot water, and the vessel drawing five foot. After half an hour's conflict had a kind of smooth on the surface, and by the Almighty's providence we got safe out of the river St Lucia. The poor creatures who had left us, some with only a shirt and a pair of drawers, travelled along shore, and we made the best of our way to the northwind . . . " (As will be seen later there may have been a more sinister reason why the nine men abandoned the boat once they believed themselves to be near civilisation.)

The long tribulations of the survivors of the *Dodington* were now to end as abruptly as they began. Here is the account as given by Jones.

"Tuesday 20th. Pleasant Gales & fair Wea^r. At 5 P M being abreast of The S° Point of Delagoa Bay, Bore Away Designing to go in and Stay For Our people, Who were Travelling on Foot along Shore. At Sun Sett the S° Point of the Bay Bore S° 3 Miles the Body of the Island St Marys [[now

Inyacka Island]] S W 2 miles. The Low Land in Sight from yᵉ Masthead on the Nᵒ Side from N to N W B W Dist About 3 Leagues. After [it was] Dark Ran under an Easy Sail. Waiting for The Moon which Would be up at 10 O'Clock, Not Suspecting butt we had a Whole Night at the Rate we Were going. Sounded [& found] Ground [in] 5 Fathom, Upon Which Alterᵈ Our Course, more Northerly, Which was More off the Land. Still Shoalᵈ our Water to 2: ½ Fathom. We then Came to Anchʳ & an Hour After The Sea Broke Very Much Close to us, therefore was [Were] Obligᵈ to Weigh, tho we did Not know Where to Better Ourselvs, the Wind Blowing into the Bay, and The Only way we Could Make a Stretch was towards the Island, Where We Expected less Water. But it prove'd Otherwise; For we by deepning [deepen'd] our water Gradually to 6 Fathom, then Came too again. Att Sun Rise, the Point S E 3 Miles, the Island S W, 1 Mile. Breakers from North to N W B W. They Seem to us to be on a Spitt of Sand, & a Channell into the Bay on Each Side of it. Last Night When we Came too, it was High Water, and as the Sea Falls, it Breaks, the Sand Drying in Some places on Spring Tides. At Noon it Was Low Water, and we Found Ourselves Surrounded with Breakers. Therefore Thought [it] the Best way to go Out, the Same way we Came in; Which We did, & in going Over the Sand Where it Broke had but 10 Feet Water. When we got Over, Deepned to 6 Fathom; which We kept Along About 2 Miles Steering N W And then Came into 9 & 10 Fathom, Which Depth We had about a Mile & Soon Deepned [Shoal'd] Again to 3 & 4 Fathom for About 1 Mile. Then Came into 5 Fathom which we kept [held] About 4 Leagˢ. Then Shoalᵈ it Gradually to 3 Fathom. Steering from West to W B S & About 4 o'Clock, Came to an Anchor in 9 Fathom, Where to Our Great Joy Found Riding The Rose Gally from Bombay Commanded by Capᵗ Edwᵈ Chander.

"Wednesday April 21 1756. The First part Fair Weather, Wind Wᵗerly, Latter fresh Gales Easterly with Rain. About 11 O Clock got under Weight in Order to go Up Mahoys River, Where Capt Chandler was Trading, butt was prevented, Not having Water Enough Over the Barr. Therefore, Returned to Delagoa again, and Dispatchᵈ a Letter to Capt Chandler, Desireing him to Spare us What Necessaries we Wanted.

"Thursday 22d. Wind and Weaʳ as Before: got Some Rice for Cloaths We are [were] Treated Very Civilly by the Commanding Officers of the Rose.

"Friday 23d. Light Land and Sea Breeze and fair Weaʳ. Bought Severall Fowls: Some Rice and Hony. The Natives Stole 31 Head of Cattell [Cattle] from the Rose Gally's [People].

"Saturday 24th. . . . Bought a Great Many Fowls Some Rice and Hony. Have a Great Number of the Natives on Board with [their] there Trade.

"Sunday 25. Light Land and Sea Breezes with pleasent Weaʳ.

"Monday 26. . . . Near Noon About 300 of the Natives Came To Capt Chandler Banksale & Drove off 66 Head of Cattell [Cattle] which he had Purchase'd [& paid for]: Which We on Board Observing, Landed as Soon As possible and Pursue'd the Robbers About 3 Miles, but Could not Gett Sight of them. Therefore not Thinking it prudent to pursue them any further, Return'd.

"Upon Our First Arrival [heard] found Capt Chandler was up in the Country About 60 Miles [[here someone has scratched out the sentence "that I could have no answer from which in four days" which gives an idea of how far inland Captain Chandler had gone]]. Therefore Dispatched One [a Letter] to him, Informing him of Our Misfortune, & at the Same Time the Behaviour of the people, [during our Stay on Bird Island] desiring [and desired] him to Assist us to gett [in getting back] the Honourable Companys Money: [and] which if [we] Effected [it] to Grant a passage to my Self Mr Collett Webb Yates and McDowell and myself to Bombay.

"The Misfortune Above Mentioned Openᵈ the 7 day after The Letter was Sent, and having Receivᵈ no answer Conjecturᵈ from the Behaviour of the Natives, that the Letters Might be Stoppᵈ or that it Might not be well with Capt Chandler. Therefore I proposed going up Mahoy's River with Our Boat the Next Morning: Which we did, and About 20 Miles up meet [Met] Capt Chandler Comeing down in his Boat very Ill wth a Fever. He told me my Letter Came Safe to Hand Which he Answerd Immediatly, and was Very Much Surprizd I had not Receivᵈ it. Howsoever we found afterwards that the Bearer was afraid to Venture Near the Vessel After what had happend The 3ᵈ day we meet [Met] Capt Chandler We Gott [return'd] on Board, and Soon Afterwards wᵗʰ some [the] assistance of some of his People took the Treasure And Plate out of the [our] Sloop, and put it on board the Rose Gally: for which Capt Chandler gave me a Bill of Lading."

Here it is as well to pause and consider the situation. Once he has arrived at Delagoa, Jones's account becomes all but incomprehensible for two reasons. The first is that at no stage does he mention in his daily record that company treasure and plate – other than the one box which was partially plundered – had been recovered and brought from Bird Island. The second is that he does not mention that at some stage he and Webb, at least, left the *Happy Deliverance*, presumably to quarter aboard the *Rose,* but also because of a row with the men in the smaller ship. Indeed, Webb recalls that Jones had to go with armed men to recover the treasure from the sloop. Concerning this last he writes: "After staying about three weeks, we saw a small country boat coming up the river, which brought three of our people, who left us at river St Lucia, and they informed us the other six were remaining on the other side of the bay of Delagoa, waiting the opportunity of a boat to bring them over. Here Mr Jones, Collet, and myself, thought this would be the properest place to secure the treasure, packets and other effects. In order to which, we enticed four or five of our men on shore, and secured two more on board the Snow [[*Snow*, the name of a vessel. Webb does not say where she came from or what part she played in the main story.]] This done, Mr Jones went with Capt Chandler's pinnace manned and armed, and took all the money, plate, and packets he could find, and brought them on board the Snow, in order to deliver them on our arrival at Madras. The people left in the sloop, being afraid we should pay them another unwelcome visit, took an opportunity of getting away in the night.

In his last entry dated Sunday May 2 1756, Jones refers to the incident in the following words: Three of the people Arriv'd from the Sᵒ Side of The Bay Where they Left the Rest of those that would Not Venture Over St Lucia Barr. They Remained there till the Sloop Sailed Which was 10 Days After the Arrival of the 3 Before Mentioned. They all Got on Board of her Alive, but Soon After 2 of them died, the Rest in a Bad State of Health. Theire Stay was but Short Where they Took the people in before they putt to Sea, in Order to go to Johanna; but After being at Sea, 5 or 6 Days found themselves off River St Lucia and 4 days Afterwards we Met them as we [were] was going out in the Rose Galley; within the Outer Barr of Delagoa. They had on Board After my Self Mr Collett & Webb. (the) 2 Navigators, who often told me on the Island they was As Capable of Conducting the Sloop as I was; those Were Powell and Chisholm but Finding Themselves Mistaken in [their] there Capacitys, Sold her [[the Happy Deliverance]] to Capt Chandler for 500 Rupees the Carpenter Took a Note for the Same payable at Bombay. While this Business was Transacting was Laying at Anchor A Little Within the Outer Barr, Waiting for wind to go Over, Which we got The Second day, And After a Passage [[The *Happy Deliverance* sailed in company with the galley on this voyage]] of 25 days Arrived in Morandavia Road on the Island of Madagascar, and 2 days After Capt Hutchinson [[Captain Norton Hutchinson, a previous captain of the *Dodington*]] in the Caernarvon Anchorᵈ here, Who Favours me with a passage to Madras where the Honble Companys Treasure and Packett is Consigned to, Who has also favoured all the people With a passage being 15 in Number my Self Include'd and all that's Now Living, Except Powell, who Some Time before the Caernarvon Sailed, Secrete'd himself in the Country, To Keep Out of Captⁿ Hutchinson's way, who Declare'd he would Take him With him. Mr Collett is One of the Number that Died." Others dead included Gilbert Chain, Henry Sharp and one of the artillerymen.

* * *

By November 1755, while the *Dodington* survivors were battling for survival on Bird Island, Robert Clive arrived in Bombay aboard the *Stretham,* eager to begin his campaign. On November 27 the Company committee at Bombay Castle wrote to the committee at Fort St George: "We hope as the *Dodington* separated from them [[the remainder of the squadron]] shortly after their departure from St Jago your next will bring the welcome news of her having got well to your place.

"Robert Clive Esq, has the king's commission as lieutenant colonel and is appointed by the Honourable Company Deputy Governor of Fort St David, and to succeed Mr Pigot in your government, took his passage and arrived here on the *Stretham*."

While in Bombay and London the Company officers cheerfully assumed that the *Dodington* had arrived safely and was still at their disposal, there was increasing concern at Fort St George as to her whereabouts. Her chests of silver, her cargo of guns, and the 200 soldiers on board were all desperately needed – the first to pay the Company soldiers, the latter for the defence of the Fort itself, particularly as Clive's return to India almost certainly indicated renewed hostilities. Fort St George's proximity to the French stronghold of Pondicherry also made a strong military contingent in the fort most desirable.

On February 4, 1756, the concern of the Fort St George committee over the ship's fate became evident in the committee minutes. The committee noted: "Three Letters from Colonel Adlercron as enter'd in the Book of his Correspondence No. 13, 14 & 15, Read, assuring us of his own and the whole Regiment's Zeal and readiness to act for the Company's Service ... And desiring a Supply of Money for the Subsistence of the Regiment; Captn Forde, the Paymaster having represented the want of it by the Dodington's not being Arrived."

At Fort William, too, the arrival of the *Dodington* was eagerly awaited for the same reason. The committee there found itself heavily out of pocket, and urgently needed a large amount of money to be shipped to them from Fort St George by the *Dodington*. (Although the ship carried only the five chests of silver with army pay, there were plans to use her around the coast if need be.) The Fort William committee had already written to London on December 8, 1755 acknowledging the receipt of 135 chests of treasure containing 288,000 Madras rupees and 792,000 Arcot rupees; but had noted "We are apprehensive we shall be under the necessity of borrowing money to begin our purchases of the next season unless the gentlemen of Fort St George send us a very large consignment by the *Dodington*."

Their concern became openly echoed by Mr George Pigot and his committee in Fort St George. Minutes in the *Diary and Consultation Book, Military Department of Fort St George* notes: "As by the long Stay of the Dodington and the receiving no news of her; there is reason to apprehend some Accident may have happen'd, it is Agreed to dispatch a Pattamar express to Bombay to desire the Gentlemen of the Select Committee to open any Packets directed for us and send us two Copies by the first Conveyances, of the Advices intended Us by that Ship and of the Instructions they may have received on the same Subject ..." Though at times the company's bureaucratic procedures must have seemed hopelessly complicated the need for duplication of documents is clearly illustrated here.

It must have been cold comfort for Mr Pigot when he received a letter from the Board of Directors in London in late March telling him that the *Dodington* had been unable to carry all her cargo and that twenty tons of cordage had been put aboard the *Pelham* for his Fort.

What Pigot desperately needed by now were guns and men. On May 7, 1756 he wrote yet again to Bombay concerning the *Dodington*. This time his letter implored the head of council there, Richard Bourchier, to send "as many as you can spare" of brass six pounder cannon, and as many of the twelve pounders "landed in Bombay the year before" as he could.

Three days later Pigot again held council and expressed his fears of renewed hostilities in the light of his depleted forces. The minutes read: "The Delawar who touch'd at the Cape bringing no news of the Dodington it is much to be fear'd She will never be heard of. The want of the Reinforcements intended us by her, more particularly the Royal Company of Artillery would be indelibly felt in case the War should break out, the Detachment now at Fort St George under the Command of Captain Hislop being insufficient for the Number of Field Pieces intended to be carried on Service with the Regiment. It is Agreed [...] to write by express Pattamar to the Select Committee of Bombay requesting that they will Send hither as many of the King's Artillery and other Reinforcements which came out with Colonel Clive as they can possible [*sic*]

Spare."

Pigot waited impatiently until May 17 when *HMS Kent* anchored in the roadstead bringing him the secret committee packet for which he had written in late February. *Kent* had been dispatched by Admiral Watson, and as soon as she had handed over the packet Pigot called a council meeting. The *Kent* also bought a letter from Robert Clive telling him that he could not spare a single man to reinforce Fort St George.

Pigot seems to have been involved in a protracted cover-up to keep from the board in London the true nature of the strength of Fort St George, having allowed its strength to slip miserably below the safety line. His letters from Fort St George become increasingly flustered. The Fort St George records show that a letter was sent on July 20 to Roger Drake, the president of council in Fort William. Pigot's committee wrote, "Several unlucky circumstances have concurr'd to reduce our forces to a *much less number than our honourable masters can be apprized of* viz:

By the disappointment of the *Dodington*	200
Detained at the west coast	100
Detained at Bombay	300
Aboard the Squadron in lieu of sailors	280
Detachment sent to Fort William	200"

Again on August 24 Pigot wrote to Bombay insisting that he could not continue in the Company's interest unless he was sent men and munitions urgently. His letter ends, "Before this reaches you we doubt not you will have been informed by the Rose Galley, of the unfortunate loss of the Dodington on the Island of Chaos in July 1755. Fifteen of her Crew that were saved arriv'd here on the Carnarvon." Pigot was clearly taking the opportunity to underline the fact that as the ship was lost he could no longer even dare hope for reinforcements from anywhere other than Bombay. By incredible coincidence Robert Clive, who had fate treated him differently for the second time in his life, might well have perished on that desolate rock pile in Algoa Bay, also arrived in Fort St George on the very day that the *Caernarvon* dropped anchor. Mr Jones at once hurried ashore to tell his story and deliver the treasure and packets he had guarded with his life.

In October Clive mounted a major expedition from Fort St George to regain Bengal which had fallen to the French. In his letter to Bombay informing Bourchier of Clive's intentions Pigot added "When you add to this draft [[of soldiers Clive took from Fort St George]] the number of two hundred and fifty men sent before to Bengal under the command of Major Killpatrick above two hundred of the regiment which are embarked for the service of the ships, and our loss by the Dodington you may judge, gentlemen, that situated as we are close to the capital establishment of the French [[Pondicherry]], we are but insufficiently furnished for the defence of the Company's own establishment upon this coast ... "

While the great strategies were being formed and Clive waited to mount his expedition to Bengal, Jones was busily explaining to George Pigot and his committee what had become of the ship to which they had looked for so much help. On August 8, 1756, several days before Pigot sent his dispatch to Bourchier, and only a week after arriving at Fort St George, Jones wrote an account of the wrecking intended both for Pigot and the directors in London. Apart from telling of the wrecking, the stay on the island, and the behaviour of the crew, Jones made two remarkable entries in this version which are ignored in both of his other accounts. He said that he had found a chest of wrought plate (something which might have been deduced from his earlier description of how the men fought over wrought plate). This was no doubt that referred to in the manifest as belonging to Charles Boddam esquire of Fort St George. He also said that he had found the army silver chest, and that he had found and saved the company's packets. Jones wrote, "The same day found the King's and honourable Company's Pacquetts which gott up, and opened the Papers to dry immediately, tho' at that time must own had no Reason for doing so. However, upon consulting Mr Collett what must be done with them, it occurred to me that it would not be impossible to build a Boat out of the Wreck, if Providence should direct us to find some Tools."

From the India Office records it seems that Jones saved all but a handful of the packets. In writing he further "desired" "that the Board will receive and give him a Discharge for a Chest of Treasure, a Box of Plate and a Lady's Watch which were saved from the Wreck."

According to the East India Company records the treasure, plate and watch were "received into the Company's Treasury." It was also recorded that "The said Mr Evan Jones and Mr William Webb, late 3rd Mate of the *Dodington*, being destitute of means to support themselves at present, and the Court of Directors having approved of the assistance which was given to the officers of the Lincoln in the year 1749 under the like Circumstances, Agreed that Eight Pagodas per month be allowed to each of them until they can procure their passage to Europe or otherwise provide for themselves."

News of the loss of the *Dodington* did not reach the directors in London until late in 1756. Until then Captain Hallett had been conducting the ship's business on the assumption that she had arrived safely, as the following items in the Company records show.

"The bearer Elizabeth Young says her husband is on board the *Dodington* and was impressed into service at Gravesend, if it be so you will see it in the captain's disbustments [[disbursements]] that I left at your office, then desire you will let her have the absence. Your most humble servant John Hallett. November 10, 1755."

"Received this 11th day of November 1755 of the owners of the ship *Dodington* the sum of £1.15s being one month's wages due to James Young belonging to the said ship. I say received by virtue of a letter of attorney to me, Elizabeth Young."

There is also a note of a payment of £10 made on April 23, 1756, to Edward Walsby being salary due to Captain Samson.

However by November 6, 1756, the directors and owners knew that the *Dodington* had been lost. On that day there is a receipt which reads: "Paid carpenter Richard Topping £4, being one months wages this being paid to Elizabeth Pilgrim by virtue of letter of attorney as Topping is now on the *Caernarvon*." The receipt book also records that John Yates had been saved and was aboard the same ship.

Chapter 5

Probably the most truthful, and certainly the most extraordinary account of the *Dodington* wreck is given in Jones's secret document. Both the "official" versions which he and Webb kept are glossy accounts suggesting that in general officers and men worked together for their common survival, with only minor incidents occurring in the later stages of their ordeal. A far different impression is given by Jones in his *A Narrative of the Peoples Behaviour on Bird Island,* Again it is wise to examine this in some detail. It begins "Which I Should have Remark'd in my Journall, but durst not, having no place to Secrete my papers but lay Exposed to Every One, and was Inspected into Daily by Several So that if I had mentioned any thing disagreeable to them, Should not have Been Suffer'd to keep a Journal att all.

"July 17th [[The day of the wrecking]] As Soon as it was Day Light, we all Assemble'd together, And for Some time only Bewail'd our Misfortunes. At Length being Roused [awaken'd] by the dismall prospect that Appeared before us. Some went to See how The Land lookd further in the Country, while the Others that Stayed With me desired I would Still Continue their Officer, and they would Obey me in all Respects, and Should Entirely Rely on my Superior Judgement to gett them of this dismall Place, being Informed by Those who went to look Round and Return'd in a few Minutes that We Were on an Island 2 Leagues from the Main. I told them they Might depend on my Assistance in all Respects and that there was Not Time to be lost, Our Situation Requiring us to be dilligent in Looking About for provissions & for Subsistance during our Stay here, which I Thought would be a Month at Least, before Every Body Would be Able to Travel. Accordingly, Sett Out and Soon Found Several Usefull Things As Inserted in my Journal, but before Night Most of Those that was Able to Work was Drunk and Rosenburry So Bad that had I not Accidentally Seen him Lying Amongst the Wreck And Call'd for Assistence to gett him up he must Infallibley have been drowned, the Side [[presumably *tide*]] having Flow'd Over part of him when we got him up, for Which Piece of Service before we Left the Island he as Often Came Close to me and Laughed in my face by way of Derision, knowing very Well I durst Not Correct him, all the Villains having Taken Theire Oaths to Stand by One Another in Opposition to the Officers, And if Either of us Offer'd to Strike any of them, three or 4 Was to Fall on him and Beat him heartily.

"Howsoever before it Came to the pass, they Obey'd me for a fortnight, by which time their was Some prospect of the Boats Going One, the keel and Steem [[stem]] being Finished; but before any more was done the Carpenter fell Sick, but by his Discourse as I found Soon Afterwards, only feign'd himself So, for Missing him from Work, Enquired after him, And was Inform'd he was Not well. Upon W^ch Information Mr Collett & Self went to Condole with him, we found him in the Cooks Tent Broiling himself a Rasher of Salt pork. I Ask'd him how he did, adding I was Sorry for his Indisposition, hopeing he would Soon be better. Yes Answer'd he that May be for Your Own Good; but I Can See how Things are Going. Your 3^d in Counsell Mr Bothwell Can be Attended On, but I may Die and be damn'd before You'll Offer mull'd Wine or any Thing Else to me; but Damn Me If I'll bee Used so. I Can See Well Enough Which Way things Are going, but I'll be damn'd if I have not a Fair Understanding before I do a St[r]oke More. Here I Interrupted him, and Told Him I thought he had gone far Enough, till he Explained himself; That I did not Understand What he Meant by Saying, he Saw how Things go. I then Asked him if he Saw Any Clandestine proceedings by Any of the Officers or any Body Else; to Which he Answer'd No, that if he did that we Should Soon know it, for Damn me if I'll be flung By the Best of You. I answer^d in my Turn, that believe^d no Body Intended to fling him as he Call'd it; therefore was Sorry to See him prejudiced Against Mr Collett & Self, because we Assisted a Sick person; Adding that As Soon As we heard of his being Out of Order, Came to Condole with him, And he Should find Either of us Very Ready to do any Thing Conducive to his Health & hoped that his present disorder was Only a Cold, Which a Little hot Wine going to Bedd would Carry off. To this he Answered in the Surly Manner as before, Saying he would have a fair Understanding before he Would do a Stroke More. Upon Which Mr Collett & I left him, and Walked together to Try if we Could guess The Reason of Such Behaviour and the Only Conjectures we Could putt on it Was his Incapacity to Build the Boat, and Some Time Afterwards, found we Were quite Right in Our Opinion, for he did not know how the Transum peice of the Searn [[stern]] was to be Fixt. He Continued Sulkey 2 days & the 3^d day, went to Work Again, Which I was Very Glad to See Making no doubt if the Would Work that We Should compleat One to Serve Our Turns.

"Soon after this Dan^ll Ladoux who was Capt^s Steward on Board the Doddington Occationed fresh disputes, by Insisting upon keeping what Pork he or his Mess Mates Pick^d up to themselve's, Which was Contrary To my Orders; and the day this dispute Arose Upon, he had Given Orders to the Cook Not to dress pork for two of the Matrosses, [[gunner apprentices]] Who was at Work with me, all the Morning on the Wreck, because they had not Brought any for Themselves. The Cook Obey'd his Orders, so that When we was Call'd to dinner, the 2 beforementioned had Nothing to Eat; therefore Made their Complaint to Me; at the Same time Inform'd Me how it happen'd Upon which I Took Ladoux to Taske, Asking him by What Authority he Order'd no Victuals to be dress^d for the two men. He Answer^d there was Orders given to the Cook by Mr Collett that What Pork he Brought to the Tent Should be Used Only for his Own Mess, Therefore he thought he had as good a Right to Keep what he Pick^d up, And for the Future None but his Own Mess Should Tast a Bitt of What he Save'd. All that he Say^d was Confirmed by his Mess Mates, And in the Most Insolent Manner that Can be Imagine'd.

"Mr Collett Declared he Never gave any Such Orders, And I am Very Certain there was no Such Orders given to the Cook by any officer but my Self, Concerning the Pörk; (And those Were) if there Should be any difference in the peices he took to dress, that I Expected the Best. This was told to all the People Imediatly, who thought Themselves Very ill Used. Therefore took the Method beforementioned to Convince me there was No difference to be made, Which gave me no Manner of Concern. However there Behaviour Shew^d I Should be a person of Very Little Consequence in a Short Time, if the Carpenter went on with his Work, but while they would Allow me to have any Command Over Them was detrimined to Exert my Authority. Therefore Insisted That Every Body Should be Carefull in picking up all the pork they Could Find, and deliver it to Mr Collett, who was Made Store Keeper, in Order that proper Care Should be Taken of it for the good of the whole. Ladoux Swore Damn him if he would Pick up Another Piece, while he was on the Island. Adding he Would Always have as good a peice of Pork as I. Being Talk^d to in this Manner by One who a few days before Attended on Me, Provoked me to Strike him two or 3 Slaps in the Face, Which had a Very good Effect, he being quit Silent Afterwards, And he and the Rest went o Work with me on the Wreck.

"Soon After this the Carpenter, and The Rest of the people was Informed by Bothwell, that the Treasure & Wrought Plate was Not to be Shared. Upon which Information Mr Collett & I was Call'd the greatest Rogues in the World, & Every One Swore it Should be Shared, and Every thing Else that Came Ashore there belong^d To Who it would. After Our days Work was Over and Every Body mett in the Tent to Supper. The Carpenter Asked me When the money and plate Was to be Shard which Surprized me greatly. Howsoever finding they Were Resolved to Share it, thought it Needless to deny my Intentions, Especially Since I found that Some I thought I Could Trust, proved false; And Indeed Bothwell was the Last person I should have Suspected being One Who Came on Board ye Doddington with a Design to Settle in India. Besides he Lay Under Some Obligations to me, for being Sick Most of the Time we Were at Sea, he had Every thing my Cabing Afforded for his Nourishment.

"Therefore Told them that Neither the money Or Plate Should be Shar^d but Delivered up to the Proper persons, when We Came to India. He then Asked me what was to be done with those Blocks I had Taken so Much Pains to Tarr, to Which I Answer'd I knew them Blocks to be of the Greatest Consequence to His Majestys Ship, And Consequently to the Hon Company whose Service I was Now in, Therefore it behoved me as an Officer to Take Care of Every thing that Might be of Consequence to the Company, Especially Such things as Was in Our power to Take with us, Which I Should do to the Utmost of My Power, and any Man that would offer to prevent them Carrening Blocks going into the Boat, I Should look upon him Ever Afterwards to be an Enemy to his Country, and an Unfit person to be Employ^d in the Service. We Were Now in. In Answer to this Chisholme, and the Rest of the People, damn the Kings Ships & Blocks, Asking Me What Either of them was to them, And Whether I thought they Built the Boat to Carry the Kings Stores of the Island or themselves. At the Same Time Swore the Blocks Should not go into the Boat, Or Money Either till it was Share'd; Adding that I was a Very Honest person to Insist that the Plate Should not be Shar^d therefore it was Very plain Only Wanted to Keep it Between Collett & My Self, and that if did deliver it, that None would gett any Credit by it but Our Selves, And as We Are all Upon a Footing Now, Nothing Should go of this Island but What Would be of Service to the Whole. The Carpenter Asking Every Now and then when the Rest would permit him to Speak Who am I. What do you Make of me. Nothing. You Shall Find that Nothing Shall go in that Boat but What I think proper. This provok^d me a Good deal, therefore desired Leave To Speak Which was Granted tho' Not without many Interruptions from Chisholm & King. Notwithstanding the Airs the Carpenter Gives himself in Saying Nothing Should go in the Boat Butt What the Carpenter Approves of, I Expect I am to have the Directions of Stowing her, and if I Can putt the Carrening Blocks which Are Only 6 in Number in the Boat, without discomoding any Body, hope'd None Would have any Objections, and on the Contrary would not desire it; And as to your Shareing the Money Desire you^ll think better of it; Being of Such Consequence as am Sure will Touch Your lives. King and Chisholm Answered they knew the Laws of their Country as well as I, And they Would Run the Risque of hanging; which Ended the dispute.

"And for about a month Afterwards was Pretty Quite, When the Carpenter took upon [himself] to Find Fault with me for Taking a Boy in the Boat with me One day when I went the Off Side of the Island To Try if [I] Could See any of the Treasure. This Boy happend to be One Who assisted the Carpenter, tho Very Seldom Employ^d and at This Time Was Idle; therefore thought it no Crime to take him. He directed, his Discourse to Mr Collett Saying I might Employ my Time much Better in Fishing, than looking About for Treasure, which would be of no Service to any Body here, if he had his Will; Adding if I had been There when the Boat Went of Chain Should not have gone in the Boat, And that he had No Business with any Body that belong'd to Him. Here Mr Collett Interrupted him Saying he thought Mr Jones had a Right to Take any Body he pleased in the Boat with him, and if it was Otherwise that for his part, Should be Subject to None Else; And as to Looking for the Treasure knew it to be my duty, Adding that he would Vouch if I did not find any thing Else to Detain me, that would Bring in fish. Chisholme was Very Impertinent all this Time and Said I might Spare my Self the Trouble of Looking for Treasure, that if he Thought what was Saved Already would not be Shared that he would Take it on his Back and Throw it Over the Rocks, Where it Never Should be Seen More. The Carpenter Spoke Next Saying he was hunted; but Damn him if he Would not do the Less for it. When I Came in Brought in 10 Large Fish with me butt Could See Nothing on the Ground where I Expected to find the Ships Bottom. As Soon as I meet Mr Collett He Told me All the Above, Desireing me at the Same time Not to Take Any Notice of it, and Not to be so much with the Carpenter, Which Counsel I Took, And only Concerned my Self in Getting up Plank, and Other Things Which we wanted most. It Would be Needless to Mention the Abuses I and Mr Collett Receiv^d, dayly therefore Shall pass Over a Month Which brings me to the Time the Treasure Chest was Broke Open And 600 Pounds Taken Out by the following persons: Viz^t, Richd Topping Carpenter, Samuel Powell 5th Mate, Nath^ll Chisholme Quarter Master, Jno

King, Robt Beazley, Fore Mast Men, Jno Lester, Montross. The Person who first Found out this Peice of Villainy was Sconce, who being Curious to know the Weight of it, found it so light that Convinced him, that there Could not be much in it; and Turning the Bottom up found it had been Cut wth a Chissell, upon which discovery went To the Rest And Told them of it. At Which Peice of News, those that Broke it Open Seem^d as much Surprized at as any of the Rest, Which Was King and Beazley, who with About 8 More Mett me as I was Comeing towards the Tent, and King in the most Sorryfull manner Told me what had happened, Exclaiming all the way till we Came to The Chest Against the Villains that did it, and desire'd in a particular Manner that I would find Some Method to find who they Were. Accordingly, As Soon as I had Secured the Remaining 1600 dollors, Mr Collett and I went into the Store Tent and drew up an Oath, which I Offer'd To Take first, and then Administer it to the Others. Some Seem'd Willing, but Waited for the Carpenter to Take it first, Which he Refused, as did all the Rest. I then desire'd it might be postponed till next Sunday, That Whosever Were the Aggressors Might have an Opportunity to Return it or Carry it from Whence they Took it, Which Was agreed upon by all, Excepting the Carpenter Chisholme and Powell, who Satt Mute all the While. I Intreated them all I Could to Return the Money Again; Telling them it Could Not be kept Secrete, and that Whosoever was the Unhappy people that Took it, and persisted in keeping it, Would Answer for it with Their Lives. This had no Effect for the Tuesday following, this being Sunday. They all took their Oaths on the Bible to Stand True to One another, and Insist upon Shareing the money & Every thing that Came ashore, Belong to Whome it Would. This Information I got from Ralph Smith Which was One Who took the Oath." This incident, and the threat that Jones intended to report the men when he reached civilisation, explains the incident at the St Lucia River when the men, realising they faced summary trial and probably hanging, abandoned the boat and later tried to make away in the *Happy Deliverance*.

"Monday the Carpenter did Nothing but make a Quadrent Case for Chisholme and tho mine wanted only Repairing Could not Get it done till 3 or 4 days before we Left the Island, and then the Smith did it. The Carpenters Not Working Surprized Mr Collett and I Greatly, Especially When We Saw them all Assemble together, and Getting drunk. Therefore I and My party Which was Mr Collett Webb & Yates Midshipman, and McDoull Went to the Other Side of the Island to Try if we Could Judge what they Were About, and we Agreed in Our Opinions, that they were Chuseing Another Person to Command them, Which we Thought would be Powell. Therefore as had been told by Chisholme & Powell Severall Times, that They were as Capable as I was to Navigate the Boat, and did not want me to Command them Thought it Needless to Concern my Self with Them any More, or at least till I Saw the Event of their Consultations. The Next day as Observ^d before was Devoted to takeing theire Oaths And drinking till most of them was drunk. The Carpenter & Powell Was So Bad they were Lead or Rather Carryed to their Hammocks. Chisholm was so Bad Could not be moved so that he lay most of the Night in the Carpenters Tent, which was become Secret to me And the Others before mentioned, And was Made no Other Use of than to keep the Carpenters and Chisholms Chests in, which is quite Furring from the Use I Intended it; for when I Raised it, being for them to Work in When it Rained. Howsoever this day when it was pretty full Took the Liberty to look in, for Which presumption the Carpenter mett me at the door and Run his head in my Face, which I took no Notice off; but Walk^d of Quitely and for the Remainder of the Week lett them Go on their Own way, without Taking Notice of any thing, tho in the Interim had Rain Which Wett all the Boats Sails Rigging, and not One of them woul be at the Trouble to gett them out to dry. All this Week, they Endeavoured to Out do one Another in Behaveing Insolent to us, for I Never Mett with any of them, as was Walking Round the Island, butt Sett up a Horse laugh at me; And as my Self and the Other 4 Used to be a good deal Over at the First Tent that was Made, Which had Still one Covering Over it, they thought it to great an Indulgence, Therefore took it of. Neither I or any of us Took the least Notice of Any of their Behaviour till Sunday, When I was to propose Taking The Oath to them Again, which thought of doing as Soon as we had Dined; But was prevented by a Quarrell that happened, between Powell & King About a Fowling Peice Which was found by the Latter, who Swore if any Man Offered to Use it, besides himself he would Shoot them with it; But Recollecting himself that he .had gone a little to far, Expected The Carpenter. Howsoever After Supper, Informed them that I had heard Nothing of the Money which was Taken out of the Chest, And desired to know if any of them had, Which was Denied. I then Asked if they would follow my Example, And Take the Oath, to Which, Jn° Glass Answer^d that I Need not Trouble my Self about it any More; Adding that those that had The money would Take Care of it. I did not think this a Sufficient Answer, therefore Asked Severall by Name, which Refused, so finding it Needless to Mention it any more, drop^d that Subject, And Asked Them if they Intended to Obey my Orders any More, and if they did not Desired they would Appoint Some body Else to Take Care of the things Which Was Lying Roting, Mentioning the Sails and Rigging. Severall of them Answer'd together they Could Take Care of the things as well I Could, And King Called out the Carpenter Should Command them, Which he Refused; but at the Same Time, Seem^d well pleased that he was A Man of Such Consequence Among them. Upon his Refusing, Beazly Answered, then Mr Jones Shall Continue, but was desired to Hold his Tongue by King, Who Said he would not Obey me Without I Consulted all of them Upon all Occasions, Which I Refused, Telling them if any One of them was Capable, would not trouble my Self any More about any thing; but as they was not, Self preservation Induces me, tho Confess if had the least prospect of a Deliverance Without, Would not do it. Notwithstanding am determined Never to Consult Such a parsell of Lubers [[lubbers]] King Answered He was as good a Man as I was, and as We Were all Upon a Footing, thought it Only Reasonable they Should be Consulted, And a Great deal more of Such Discourse. Howsoever it Ended desireing I would Continue to direct them.

"About a Month After this Mr Collett Happen^d to go into the Carpenters Tent, at a Time When Chisholm & the Carpenter was drinking Some Brandy and Water, of Which they Asked him to partake; which he did and drank Success to Our Undertakings. With all my Heart Answer^d the Carpenter, and am glad we Are all Alive, that Came Ashore. This Startled Mr Collett a little, but not Seeming to Understand What he meant, Say^d it was a Very Wholesome Air Or Some Would have been dead, Eating Such Trash as we Were Obliged to do Sometimes. Yes Answer^d he I believe the Air is Very good, Notwithstanding that you may thank god, you're Alive, for not long ago, there was Some who designed to have Murther^d Mr Jones your Self, & the Other 3; Adding there was only one Mans Consent wanting, And it would Certainly [have] been done, Which was Jn° King that Refused And Say^d he would Dye first before he would Suffer it to be done. And Two days ago told me of it, I desire you^ll Keep what have told You a Secret, and When we get from hence and Come to another Place will tell you More of it, but we ever Afterwards Found him in So good a Humour, as When he told Mr Collett the Above Mentioned, So that am quite Ignorant who the Villains Are Who was to have been the Executioners.

"The Next thing we was Inform'd was That the Kings & the Honble Companys packetts was to be burnt, least it Might be Hurtful to them at Mozenbeys besides they Suspected Our papers was in it. Lester the Montross Asked Severall to Assist him to do it, but they Refused being Afraid it would be found out, And the Kings Pacquet being there, it would hang them.

"Being at Work Upon the Wreck one day Was Surprized to See McDoull Coming towards me in Great Confusion, and it was Some time before he Could Speak. At length he told me, they were Murdering Mr Collett in the Tent. I left what was About Immediately, And as was Walking Over the Island Asked him the Meaning of it. He told me that Some had been Complaining There Baggs had been Robb^d and Mr Collett Advizeing to Search all in the Tent, was Taken up by King, Saying that his Should Be Search'd first, Adding that he was the Greates thief Ashore; Which provoked Mr Collett to Strike him, And King Return^d it. When McDowel left the Tent Severall Others had got Round him Crying – Thresh him, damn him, learn him to Strike Again. Howsoever by The Time I Came it was all Over and Collett was gone from the Tent, I thought it Needless to take any Notice of it, for they were Quite Masters, and in all probability, Should have Come off no Better than Mr Collett; so Returned back to make an End of what I was About.

About a fortnight before we Left the Island a Fresh Rupture broke Out; Powell being discover[d] by one of the People with a Bottle of Brandy, Which he Knew must be Out of The Sea Stock [[to be taken on the *Happy Deliverance*]]. Therefore Came and Made his Complaint to me, tho not without Consulting the Rest first. I Sent for Powell and Told him what was laid to his Charge, which putt him in a great Passion, denying that he Ever Touch[d] it. Those who accused him durst not prove it, being desired to Hold their Tongues by King and Some More of them. Powell was Extreemly Offended, that I should Call him to Account for any Such thing, Saying he did not know a more Likelyer a person than myself to do Such a thing; Adding that One day when Every body was gone to gather Eggs, Excepting Mr Webb and my Self, we had drank out two-thirds of a Case Bottle, Which he had Found a little before Under Mr Webbs Hammock. Being Accused of a Fraud which I Never thought of provoked me So that I could [not] Help Striking him, which he Returned, and Grabbed fast Hold of me. He was Soon Undermost, and the Carpenter as Soon Informed of it, Who Came Running into the Tent, and Came Immediatly to Me, being Disengaged from Powell before he Came in, which I believe Save'd me Some Strokes from him; saying that I was the person that Stole The Brandy, – And that he knew how it was a going Some Time ago. I believe he Spoke Truth Against his Will, Now or at least Unknown to him, for I Make no doubt but his Confident gave him a drink Now and then. The Next that took Me to Task was Lester the Montross, Who asked me by what Authority I Sent for him, and Order him and the 2 Other Montrosses to Assist me, if any Body Should Attempt to take the Remain'd[r] of the Money; Adding that he would Lett me know he was My Officer, Being in the Kings Service and I Only in the Merchants. I did not think it Worth my While to Answer him, but he was going on in the Same Abusive Manner the Others Used to do, which provoked me to Call him Villain, and Told him if he did not Leave of his Abusive Language I would knock him down, with the first thing that Came in my way. But he Only laught at me Telling me I was the Greatest Villain, and wish[d] I would Offer to Strike him, he would desire no better Sport. The Usage I had Receiv[d] from the Rest before and the Abusive Language from this Scoundrell, put me past my Reason, therefore Run towards him; and he Meeting me, which I did not Observe, got the first Blow, which had not in my Power to Return, being taken hold of by Mr Collett and the Rest who parted us. By this Time Chisholm who had been out of the Tent Some Time, Came in Swaggering and Asked what Domineering was going on Now, that they would have no More of it; Adding he knew what to do With the Boat at Well as I when She was afloate. And if I wanted Any Thing to Turn Out with him he would make me Easey presently; Which Challange I did not Care to Except; but told him, if he durst Take one of the Guns, I would Meet him with Another, which he Refused. And Then the Carpenter, who Refused lickwise, but Upon Second Thought Said he Would. Accordingly went out of the Tent and I follow'd. He began to Strip himself and asked what I was for, Stick or fist; Adding he would Lett me See he was Not Afraid of his Flesh, I Said Nothing to him butt Return'd into the Tent Again; and he Followed, Asking me if taking 2 Guns was the way to try a Man. No Answer[d] Chisholm a Good Stick or Fist is the way. So this Fray Ended with Telling me, they did not want any more of my Commanding or Domineering Over them, and That They Were all Upon a Footing, therefore wanted no Commander. To Which I made them no answer. Neither did I Concern my Self with any Thing afterwards, till within a day the Boat was to be Launched; but There was very little to do which Made me quite Easy, and from this Time Would Mess no More with the Carpenter. And indeed Should not have Eat with him at all, if I thought he would have Behaved in the Manner he has done; for when I divided the people into two Messes Thought by Taking all the Officers into Mine, there Would be no danger of the Rest of the People doing any thing Contrary to our Will. But it happen[d] I Made Choice of the greatest Scoundrells. I Enjoy[d] Being

The Sea Bed: above: an octopus can be distinguished in amongst the copper plate.
below: explosive shells appear indistinguishable from rocks to the inexperienced
eye (centre foreground); more copper plates lower left.

in a Mess by Our Selves Greatly, and so did the Rest of my Mess Mates; Notwithstanding they were Obliged to Cook for themselves, and Often 3 days before we Could get the Kettle to Make Broth, which was the Best of Our Food at That Time; it being Mostly Employ^d for the Carpenters. And if at any Time it was Not, all the Rest Insisted being Served before us. The People Receiv^d their Orders from the Carpenter & Chisholm Which was to get as Much Iron as they Could, and our Method of Getting it was to Burn it Out of the Wreck, and one day When they had fired it, took the Trouble to Carry the Carrining [[careening]] Blocks I had got up and Tarr^d and threw them in the fire. Beezley was Seen to throw one in by Yates. About 4 or 5 days before the Boat was Launchd Powell Seemd to be head Man, giving his Orders to Take the Brandy Cask and Rinch [[rinse]] them. Mr Collett Assisted to gett them out of the Tent, they being in the Place, Where we Mess, and afterwards took The Liberty of Rinching one of them out with a little fresh Water; Which Powell Observing, Damn^d his Assurance and Asked what Business he had to do that, Swearing he Should not have it, and Call^d him all the Infamous Names Could be thought of ; Swearing that None of us Shall go of the Island in the Boat, and Indeed Expected that would be the Case.

"Howsoever 2 days Afterwards the People Came To me to know if I thought proper to have the things Share'd. I Asked Them Whether they were Tantalizing me and if they did not think being Left on the Island was Not Punishment Enough without it.

"They Answered they Intended no such thing, And as to What Powell Says Signifies Nothing; Adding they Hoped Every thing Might be forgott, and that I would Take upon me the Direction as before. I Readyly Complye'd with their Request, and told Them that had no Objections to Sharing Such Things as I knew No Owners to; But as to the Treasure and Plate Could nor would not Consent to Share it. Therefore hoped they would Return what was Taken Out of the Chest, and Allow things to go in their proper Channell; which if you do, Assure you, Whats past Shall be Buried in Oblivion. They Made me no Answer, but Went to the Carpenters Tent, and in a few Minutes Return^d Again, Saying they were Determined to Share Every thing, And desired to know, What we would have done with Our Shares. Collett told Them to Lay it a One Side; but as they divided it, they Brought Ours to us which We took Care of, thinking it Better to Save so much of it. Than lett them Have it. The Money which was Taken out of the Chest [[during the previous incident]] Was Concealed in the Boat, butt they happened to be Discovered doing it, by Some of those who was not concerned who Immediately Told the Rest. So finding they were Blown took it Out Again the day Before it was Shar^d. As soon as the Money was divided the Other things Was putt up to Auction, being a Contrivance of Mr Colletts to Save the Plate, Which Otherways would have Been Run down. 2 days After this we Launched the Boat and the Next day in Getting her Out, the Grapnail Came home and She Drove Upon the Rocks; Which Accident the Carpenter Layed to my Charge, Saying that if h^e had Been Aboard it Should not been So I Asked him how he would have Prevented it; but being at a Loss for an Answer only Grumbl^d at Me. While we Were at Sea they would Often find Fault with my Carrying to Much Sail, Threatening to Cutt the Haliard, and Lett the Sail Come down. This was When we Were before the Wind and Sea, And had we not Carryed Sail to give the Boat Some Way through the Water, Would Certainly have foundred. When we went into the first port it was by Consent of Every Body; but When I proposed going out, they Objected Against it Saying it would be Time Enough 10 or 12 days hence. Howsoever the Wind Coming Fair about a week afterwards we Were Ready Sail^d. While We lay in this Port, Chisholm Always Staye'd ashore to Buy What the Natives Brought to sell, and I being a Shore one Day When a Small Elephants Tooth was Brought to the Tent, begg^d Leave to Buy it: Which Offended Mr Chisholm Greatly, and Told me I would only Spoile The Markett. Howsoever I Bought the Tooth, and Gave the man About 4 pounds of Iron for it, tho Believe Could have got it for Less, butt

---

above: Alfred
below: a howitzer breaks the surface. Just visible are the *Etosha's* rudder and propeller. The white area top left is the effect of a wave on the surface.

Chapter 6

The wreck of the *Dodington* was a cause célèbre for 100 years because it highlighted a most critical error in the charts hitherto used – that they showed the eastern South African seaboard cutting away to the north too rapidly. By turning too soon, and because of an error in judging the distance he had sailed from Cape Agulhas, Captain Samson fell into a trap he had no way of avoiding. Bird Island, nestling in the north-western corner of Algoa Bay, was first reported by Bartholomew Dias when he made his pioneering voyage round the Cape in 1488. It was first charted in 1575 when, on the orders of King Sebastian of Portugal, Manuel de Mesquita Perestrelo, drew up his roteiro of sailing instructions for rounding the Cape and sailing past Africa to India. Perestrelo wrote of Algoa Bay: "Cape Arrecife [[now Cape Recife]] is in latitude 33 degrees and a third [[only 42 minutes out from the correct latitude]]. Along this Cape on the eastern side is a great open unsheltered bay, which is called Lagoa, although I had called it before the Bay of the Wolves [[sea wolves – probably walruses]] owing to the great number I found in it. It may have a mouth ten or twelve leagues across [[the Portuguese league measured 3.197 modern nautical miles]]. On the western side there are four islets which are called of the Cross [[now St Croix]], one of them larger than the three around it, where any ship can find shelter at all times, for the bottom is clean sand with twelve and thirteen fathoms of water. In the eastern side of the bay in the same latitude lie two other [[in fact four]] that are called Chaos, because they are so flat that they cannot be seen farther off than two leagues." The island was so called well after the *Dodington* struck it, and in a British chart of 1759 was called Confused Island. This chart showed it at five degrees east of Cape of Good Hope and in latitude 34 degrees. Several other charts exist which put the island almost as far north-east as the Great Fish River.

In the fifth edition of Dunn's *Directory for the East Indies* printed in 1780 there is a long note referring to the *Dodington* disaster. "Consider the shocking account of the loss of the *Doddington* [[so spelled in this account]] Indiaman. The day at noon, before she was lost, she was in latitude by observation 35° S. and had made longitude from Cape Lagullas [[now Agulhas, southern most tip of Africa]], 12° 50′ E. They had winds from S. S. W. to S. S. E. strong gales with a large sea and altered their course at noon from E. to E. N. E. and run about 70 miles on that course, till about a quarter before one A. M. when she struck and went all to pieces in less than 20 minutes. The *Doddington's* latitude by account when she struck was 34° 6′ S. longitude made from Cape Lagullas 13° 45′ E. by carefully working their supposed run from the time she was lost. What variation they had is not known. It would be of use, not having been taken on that coast. This shocking circumstance of the loss of the *Doddington* and such a number of lives will make the skilful navigator shudder, and make him rack his invention to point out the cause of such misfortunes, and contrive how to avoid the like accidents happening for the future, by finding proper methods effectually to prevent them. The first cause of the loss of the *Doddington* seems to have been that their reckoning must have been very much ahead of the ship, occasioned by the current which runs strong to the westward, all along this part of the coast of Africa to Cape of Good Hope [[the Agulhas current]]. The second cause; that the land is erroneously laid down in our draughts, charts and books, the land lying much more to the southward than it is laid down. The charts make it trench away to the northward too quick. This is a very great error. It deceives and misleads the navigator, making him haul to the northward too soon, running him into danger. Whereas he should keep more to the East to avoid it. The third cause is that the *Doddington* made her course too much northerly. She steered E. N. E. and must at least have had 25° W. variation [[in her magnetic compass]], which is 2¾ points, with a great sea from the southward: so that he could not make her course better than N. E.] N., which was too northerly a course had she been 2° of longitude to the eastward of where she was by reckoning. The *Doddington's* reckoning seems to be very erroneous, for they had made longitude to where the ship was lost 13° 45′ E. from Cape Lagullas, and where the ship was lost is not more than 3° to the eastward of the said Cape. By the latest observations it was but 7° E. of Cape Lagullas. The variation hereabout, as well as several other parts, may be looked upon as a sure and principal guide in navigation. This unfortunate ship should be a caution for all navigators to be very cautious not to haul to the northward too soon, for the currents are very deceiving. It appears by the account of the people that were saved out of the *Doddington* that she was not the only ship that had been cast away on that island, for they saw the remains of several other ships that had been lost there: no doubt by the same cause that she was lost."

The inaccuracy of the charts has long been well documented. The Swedish naturalist Anders Sparrman noted in his book, "Here it is likewise necessary to remark, that all the maps and charts of the eastern coast of Africa hitherto known, are faulty in making the extent of it to the eastward much less than it really is, and than I found it to be in my journey over land. I am likewise sensible, that many navigators have, in the course of their voyages, taken notice of the same error; and among them Captain Cook, at the time when, being on his return from his first voyage round the globe in the *Endeavour,* he fell in with this coast unawares. Moreover, during our stay near *Sea-cow-river,* a ship was seen one evening under full sail making directly for the shore, and did not tack about till she was almost too near. I afterwards learnt at the Cape, that this was a Dutch vessel; and that from the chart she carried with her, she had not expected to come upon the coast nearly so soon, nor had she perceived it till just before she had tacked about."

Again Sir John Barrow, in his book, *Travels in South Africa,* notes: "In speaking of charts, it may not perhaps be considered unimportant to observe in this place, that the whole of the coast of South Africa, between Algoa or Zwartkops Bay, and that of De La Goa, stretches in reality much farther to the eastward (making the continent in this part much wider) than it is laid down in any of the sea-charts that have hitherto been published; by several degrees more easterly than some of them make it. To this circumstance may probably have been owing the loss of the *Grosvenor* East Indiaman, and many other ships that have been wrecked on the Kaffer coast; and by it may be explained the reason why ships, coming from the north-eastward, almost invariably fall in with the land, to the northward of Algoa Bay, a full degree or more before they make it by their observations or reckoning. Immediately beyond Algoa Bay, the coast, in the charts, is usually made to trend to the north-east, and even to the northward of this point, whereas in reality, it runs only east-north-east to the mouth of the Great Fish River or Rio d'Infante, whose latitude at this place, by repeated observations I found to be 33 degrees 25 minutes south; and from hence to the mouth of the Keiskama in the Kaffer country, the direction continues pretty nearly the same; after which, and not before, the coast begins to trend more to the northward."

Eighty-six years after the wreck, James Horsburgh, hydrographer to the East India Company, made a lengthy mention of the *Dodington* in the 1841 edition of his *Directions for Sailing to and from the East Indies.* The entry reads: "Bird Islands, in lat 33° 52′ S., lon 26°5′ to 26° 18′ E., by Capt Owen's survey, distant about 10 leagues E. ¾ S. of Cape Recif, consist of three low islands, with several black rocks above and under water, extending 4 or 5 miles nearly N. W. and S. E., and distant 6 or 7 miles from the main land. H M. Ship *Stag* examined these isles in March 1814, in search of the wreck of the *William Pitt* [[wrecked in 1813]]; entering from the westward between them and the land, she anchored within them in 17 fathoms, and passed through to the eastward between them and Cape Padron on the following day. In mid channel the least water was 12 and 13 fathoms inside the isles, and in some parts 17 and 18 fathoms rocky bottom; but sounding in the boats, the depths decreased regularly to 6 or 7 fathoms close to the main, where the ground was found better for anchorage than near the islands. Bird Island is the easternmost of them and is of round form and about a quarter of a mile in extent; the landing was found difficult on account of the rocks; myriads of birds, particularly gannets and penguins, covered the isle. The next isle about half a mile in length, called Seal Island, and the third called Stag Island, with black rocks that extend from it to the westward were all covered with seals. There are two sunken rocks surrounded by others, partly visible at low water, but in fine weather the sea probably does not break high on them at high tide; one of these isles is 2½ miles from Bird Island, and S. W. by S. from the west end of the reef.

"Doddington Rock, bearing S. W. from the centre of Bird Island, at 6 or 7 miles' distance, is in lat 33° 57′ S., lon 26° 11′ E., by Capt Owen's survey; and it was on this rock that in 1756 the Doddington [[so spelled in this account]], East Indiaman, struck in the night when steering E. N. E. There are 25 and 26 fathoms water [[150 and 156 feet]] near the East and West extremes of Bird Isles and the depths are thought to be from 35 to 40 fathoms near the Doddington Rock on the out side, which is very dangerous for ships making the land hereabout in thick weather, or in the night, more particularly if standing toward the shore when working to windward. Woody Cape is to the northward of the Bird Islands, in lat 33° 46′ S., lon 26° 14′ E.

"Cape Padron, in lat 33° 46′ S., lon 26° 25′ E., by Capt Owen's survey, bears E. N. E. from Bird Islands, but although there is a channel between these islands and the main, through which the Stag passed, as mentioned above, that might be used in case of necessity, yet it is uncertain if there be any secure anchorage inside of these islands in bad weather, on account of the bottom being rocky near them, as far as that ship explored."

A footnote to the above survey reads "This description of Doddington Rock, Bird Islands and the adjacent coast is chiefly by Mr L. Fitzmaurice, R. N. [[captain of HMS Stag]], who went in the Stag Frigate's boats to examine the isles and the channel. Although the Bird isles were surrounded with high breakers two small inlets or creeks were discovered at the west end of the easternmost isles with smooth water where the boats landed. On the beach of the main, opposite to the isles, the high surf rendered it impracticable to land and steep cliffs with sand-hills seemed to present an impenetrable barrier to the interior." (It was Fitzmaurice who found Mrs Collett's grave still clearly marked on the island during the survey.)

It is clear from the material quoted that Mr Jones's navigation was extremely poor. Whereas he believed his co-ordinates at the time of the wrecking to be 34° 30′ S. and 31° 30′ east, the Stag survey shows that the island is in fact at 33° 48′ S. and 26° 29′ E.

In the Indian Antiquary Sir Richard Temple precedes his quotation of Horsburgh's entry with the correct deduction, apparently made from his own review of the ship's course and speed, that the Dodington was not wrecked on Doddington Rock at all. The survivors of the wreck thought it struck on Seal Island: Dodington Rock seems to have been so named by those in HMS Stag. The confusion which resulted caused many expeditions searching for the wreckage to go totally awry in their efforts. Thus Temple, who adopted the spelling Doddington, and may have used it as such in some of the accounts he quoted, wrote "The Doddington must have been wrecked as a matter of fact off Bird Island, and the dangerous rocks about 6 m S. of it, now known as the Doddington Rock, must have been named at a later period."

By 1874 the importance attached to the wreck had started to fade. It was noted in Taylor's East India Directory, but at not nearly so great a length as in Horsburgh's Directions. Taylor's entry reads in part, "Bird Islands, a cluster of low rocky islets, E. ½ S., 30 m. from Cape Recife and nearly S. S. W. 5 m. from Woody Cape, were dangerous to navigation before the erection of a lighthouse on the largest of the group, which has the appearance of a ship under sail. These islands are the resort of numerous seafowl, and are covered to the depth of several feet by an inferior kind of guano. It is 33 feet above sea, 800 yds. long and 600 yds. wide. No water is found on it, save in hollows of the rocks after rain. Eggs are abundant at seasons; a very palatable vegetable, not unlike spinach, grows on it. Fish may be had in plenty ...

"Bird Island Lighthouse in lat. 33° 50′ S., lon. 26° 17′ E., is a white wooden pyramid, with a broad black belt in the middle. It stands on the S. side of the island. It exhibits two fixed white lights, 61 and 51 ft above H. W. visible 10 m. They are 18 ft apart horizontally and when directly over each other point to the Doddington Rock upon a S. W. $\frac{1}{2}$ W. bearing ...

"The Doddington and E. and W. Rocks are three dangers lying within $1\frac{1}{2}$ m. of the Bird Island Light, with it bearing between N. N. E. and E. The two former are awash and the latter has $2\frac{1}{2}$ fathoms over it, but the sea is seldom so smooth as not to break. Close around the depths are 10 to 12 fms. Between these rocks and the islands the soundings are irregular between 5 and 10 fms. During heavy weather a tremendous sea rolls over the whole of this space, producing a surf truly terrific, the sea breaking in 8 and 10 fms. water to seaward. It is necessary to give the Bird Islands dangers a wide berth in passing, since it is difficult to distinguish between the sea that breaks in 10 fms. and that which rolls over the reefs. This is one of the most dangerous parts of the coast especially to a stranger."

Chapter 7

Almost immediately after the disaster efforts were made to find the wreck of the *Dodington*, chiefly because she was believed to be a treasure ship. Strictly speaking this was not so. The East India Company's inventory shows that she carried Clive's gold, together with some 35,000 ounces of silver; but this, valuable though it was, could not really be regarded as treasure. Nevertheless, "treasure" ship or not, the *Dodington* at once became sought after, and with the progress of the years the fable of fabulous wealth on Bird Island grew. A second folk-tale has also steadily gained acceptance, that the "treasure" was buried secretly on the mainland, either by officers or crew, in the hope of returning later for the spoils.

The first effort to find the wreck was made in 1756, the year after she struck the reef. At the request of the British East India Company a Dutch dogger, a two masted bluff-bowed fishing boat, was sent from the Cape to look for the island and the *Dodington*. Sparrman said that it was widely believed that the captain deliberately returned empty handed to the Cape "without executing his commission" in the hope of returning later to find the treasure for himself. He added, "It perhaps would still pay for the labour to build a boat at *Zondags-rivier* [[now Sundays River]], with a view to search for these small islands; but in order for people coming from the sea to find them, it would be necessary that somebody should have previously observed the true latitude on the continent directly opposite them . . ."

There was even a suggestion in 1757 that the ship could be salvaged by diving on the site of the wreck. John Lethbridge, a British pioneer salvage diver who in 1715, short of money and with a large family to support, had hit on the idea of recovering valuables and treasure from sunken ships and later worked on wrecks at the Cape, asked permission from the East India Company to dive on the *Dodington*. To carry out his dives he had invented a "diving engine" which he described in a letter to the *Gentleman's Magazine* in September 1749, eight years before his application to the East India Company. "To recover wrecks from the sea," he wrote, "the first step I took towards it was going into a hogshead, upon land, bung'd tight, where I stay'd half-an-hour without communication of air . . . I found I could stay longer under water than upon land . . . you have the following description of the engine it is made of wainscot perfectly round, about six feet in length, about two feet and a half in diameter at the head and about eighteen inches at the foot, and contains about thirty gallons; it is hooped with iron hoops without and within to guard against pressure. There are two holes for the arms, and a glass about four inches in diameter, and an inch and a quarter thick to look thro' . . . two air holes upon the upper part, into one of which air is conveyed by a pair of bellows, both of which are stopt before going down to the bottom . . . it requires 500 weight to sink it." It was in this curious machine that Lethbridge proposed to tackle the treacherous reefs of Bird Island.

Lethbridge's request to the East India Company for sponsorship and permission to dive on the *Dodington* was dated June 19, 1757, and was written only eleven days after the *Public Advertiser* carried the first public account of the wrecking of the ship on its front page. Posted from his home at Newton Abbot in Devon, Lethbridge's letter read:

"Sir, I having seen in the published papers that the *Dodington*, Indiaman, was sometimes since wrecked on one island about 34 south and presuming she had a considerable quantity of treasure on board, I therefore take the liberty of troubling you with this, to request you to signify to the honourable East India Company that I am ready to serve them, in the recovery of the treasure lost, in case they are inclined to contract therefore, and if so, I should be glad to be

61

informed what quantity of treasure was on board, and of what it consisted and what distance the ship was wrecked from the Cape of Good Hope, (where I have been on a diving expedition for the Dutch East India Company). I am the person that waited on you in March 1755, in order to contract for a diving expedition to the Isle of May, but was prevented, by a contract subsisting with one Mr Mill, which contract, I apprehend expires next spring, at which time, I should readily contract, for the recovery of the treasure, lost in the *Princess Louisa;* your answer hereto will vastly oblige. Your most humble servant, John Lethbridge."

The company must have been startled by this request from a man in his eighties. Their decision that he should not be allowed to undertake the expedition was a wise one: according to the church register at Wolborough, near Newton Abbot, Lethbridge was buried on December 11, 1759, two years later.

It is said that at the time of his death Lethbridge had recovered some £100,000 worth of valuables from Dutch and English wrecks all over the world.

A spark of flame later appeared through the smokescreen of the treasure fable in the extraordinary activities and writings of a Dutchman, Gert van Bengel, who was later dispatched to a lunatic asylum in Holland. His dabblings in the *Dodington* affair, the most colourful and fantastic of all, were recorded with a fair amount of cynicism in the *Cape Monthly Magazine* in July 1860. Though it is a long and rambling story no account of the *Dodington* could be truly complete without it. Here, in part, is the text: "Most of us may have heard of "Woody Cape" but, perhaps, few are aware of its exact locality, and fewer still, of the strange traditions connected with the place, and so generally current amongst the neighbouring farmers.

"Forming the north-eastern horn of Algoa Bay, it is simply remarkable when seen from a distance to seaward as a uniformly dark and isolated prominence, with little distinguishable feature, and only conspicuous in contrast with the weary monotony of the extensive tracts of bare white sandhills which form the coast on either side of it.

"It is only when seen from a position close in shore that its stiff and beetling crags wildly strike the eye, especially as viewed under the rapidly changing shadows of sunset, when the seaward face of the precipice presents a huge, huddled mass of fanciful and grotesque shapes, ever varying in form and position.

"On shore, and underneath the cliff, which, at low water, is for the greater part accessible from the beach, the wildness and grandeur of the scene is even increased. High above the rugged rock and shingle of the beach, beetles the perpendicular front of a dark-brown decayed sandstone, covered at the summit with a dense impenetrable jungle of brushwood, matted together by long yellow ropes of *cynanchum*, and the interminable twigs of the treacherous *wacht een beetje* [[still a common Afrikaans name for a thorn bush now called *wag 'n bietjie*, which means *wait a bit*]].

"For upwards of a mile in the back-ground, and as far as the eye can reach, on either side, the land consists of a fine and beautifully white sand, not of an unvaried level, as in Table Bay and other parts of the southern coast, but swelling into huge masses, and forming steep and conical sandhills (some of them rising to the height of three of four hundred feet), continually altering in form and locality, particularly with the strong westerly gales which whirl in amongst them and sweep the eddying sand, in huge clouds and columns, far and wide. Above high-water mark, a stream of clear, fresh water, about the thickness of a man's body, is seen to issue from a fissure in the cliff, and mingle with the spray beneath ...

"The beach is everywhere thickly strewn with driftwood; and the presence of numerous fragments of wrecks adds, if possible, to the interest and wild solitude of the scene, – such as portions of a burnt hull, a shattered boat, broken oars, battered spars, sheaves of blocks, and other ships' furniture abundantly scattered about, as also the wave and weather-beaten fragment of a life-buoy, jammed high up in a crevice in the cliff, and which all seem to point to many an unknown tale of hardship and disaster.

"We have indited these descriptive remarks, in order the better to introduce to the notice of the reader a curious little volume ... *Zonderlinge lotgevallen van Gerrit Cornelis van Bengel, vooral aan de Zuid Oost Kust van de Kaap de Goede Hoop in de Jaren* 1747–1758. *Uit nagelatene Papieren bewerkt en uitgegeven door Mr. Simon Proot, J.U.D. Gedrukt by de Gebroeders van der Post. Utrecht* 1860 . . .

"Gerrit van Bengel, it appears, was born in Arnhem, in 1715; and following the profession of his father (who in early life had landed with William III, at Torbay, as a trumpeter), he soon rose to the rank of corporal in the Dutch East India Company's service, in which capacity he arrived in Table Bay, in the company's ship *Veldhoen*, in 1747, with the pay of twelve guilders per month . . . According to the article van Bengel was frugal, but of a visionary turn of mind which made his fellow soldiers question his general sanity. Then a chance meeting with a shipwrecked sailor in 1757, when he had been ten years in the Cape, fanned the flame of his imagination afresh. "The ill-fated *Dodington*, laden with treasure and merchandise from England, had been wrecked off Bird Islands, in 1755" the article continues, "His new acquaintance communicated to him the strange, eventful story of the shipwreck – expatiated in glowing terms on the treasures which the ship's officers had buried on the island, on a spot unknown to the men, for fear of indiscriminate plunder and eventual mutiny amongst them. A romantic adventure, during the stay on the island, interested van Bengel still more. Three of the ship's crew, and amongst them the narrator himself, had gone out fishing one day, in one of the *Doddington's* boats, [[so spelled in the original]] in the direction of the opposite coast; and venturing too near the surf, which was rolling high at the time, their boat had capsized, and he and another sailor (being both good swimmers) had escaped on the not distant shore. Here he remained for a whole day, when he succeeded in again reaching the ship with the boat, which had happily been cast on the shore. While there, he had seen curious sights. Perceiving a stream of water issuing from a rock covered with dense bushes, and overhanging the cliff, he had clambered up to slake his thirst, when he noticed a large number of bags, evidently containing money, and further appearances of treasure in another opening close by; but the fear of being cut off by the rushing tide, which was already setting in strongly, had made him desist from further explorations.

"Gert van Bengel's mind was now made up for immediate action. He petitioned the then Governor, Ryk Tulbagh, to be discharged from the Company's service, and to be made a burgher, by reason of his having done duty for ten years. It was absolutely requisite to obtaining a discharge, in those days, that the petitioner should state what handicraft he intended following. This puzzled him for awhile, as he had been all his life a soldier. At last, he fixed on tailoring,–not that he understood it, or intended pursuing it at all; but his object was only to seize the first favourable opportunity for escaping in some vessel from his thraldom, as, with the ostensible rights of a freeman, he would still be subject, in those despotic times, to several restrictions and disadvantages,–such as his not being allowed to leave the limits of the colony, and his running many risks of being more or less arbitrarily compelled to resume his old duties of corporal, on pain of deportation.

"His request was, without much difficulty, acceded to, for, fortunately for him, he had just hit upon an employment which was then in very great demand at the Cape. Orders for habiliments of every description soon poured in from all directions, but the pseudo tailor slyly craved a little leisure-time, for providing, as he said, the neccessary tools, furniture, and material; and one fine morning, while, no doubt, the good, easy burghers of Cape Town, in their artless simplicity, were picturing to themselves the ex-corporal perched, pagoda-like, on his elevated board, and vigorously plying his needle, or with sure-guiding hand propelling his steaming goose over their fine Leyden broadcloth,–the rogue lay snugly hid amongst the casks in the hold of the *Zwaardvisch*, an outward-bound East Indiaman, which was just about weighing anchor in Table Bay. After some twenty-four hours' confinement, Gert ventured from his skulking-place, with his *Burger Privilegie* in hand, to show, at all events, that he was no common deserter. It was now too late to send him on shore again, and there was therefore no alternative but to make him work his passage as a sailor, which, of course, he was very willing, though unaccustomed, to do. On doubling Cape Agulhas, the ship encountered a fearful storm, which she only escaped after losing part of her mizen-mast, and suffering otherwise very considerably; so that, some days after, when she was sailing in fair weather between the coast and the Bird Islands (for hugging the shore was then much more common than at present), the captain, mindful of the long voyage still before him, thought it prudent to anchor under the lee of the islands, to repair the damage which the storm had occasioned.

"What an unlooked-for concurrence of events for Van Bengel! That he should ever actually view so near, and while at anchor, the spots which his sailor-friend had so fascinatingly described to him, had scarcely ever crossed his glowing imagination. He rubbed his eyes in wonderment. But, surely, he was perfectly awake. And *there* lay the Bird Islands, quite close to him; and yonder, some miles further, his peering eye could plainly discern the opposite coast, with its broad belt of sandhills stretching from the west, and that sudden dark-looking break, the very spot so minutely described to him by the stranger . . .

"A delay of some ten or twelve days at the Bird Islands was anticipated by the captain, for effecting his repairs. This gave the sailors an opportunity of visiting the cluster, on the south-east side of which they found a large anchor and an iron gun, which, from its fine state of preservation, left no doubt of having belonged to the *Doddington*. Van Bengel was marvellously alert in poking about for appearance of the hiding-place of the ship's treasure: but he was soon satisfied that the search would be a hopeless one, for nearly the whole island was covered with a guano crust, to the depth of several feet, and all that he found was gannet eggs innumerable, remains of muskets, spars, and other pieces of wood intermixed with the débris of a ship's forge, and such-like articles.

"In his eagerness for spoil, he partly opened a low mound, which, however, he soon discovered to be a human grave.

"The fruitless result of his explorations here, now unmistakably pointed, he thought, to that other treasure spot on the opposite coast (and which, from our description, the reader will, ere this, have identified as Woody Cape), as the locality where his golden visions would certainly be realized.

"How, however, could he accomplish that Herculean task, for the distance was considerable; and he was aware, as we have seen, of the dangers connected with an attempt to land on the coast. To get the captain's consent to so fool-hardy an expedition, which would require a boat's crew that could be ill-spared at that busy time, was out of the question. Besides, even with permission, what sailor would risk his life to accompany him for such a purpose. But the indomitable ardour which possessed him left no obstacle unsurmountable to his mind. He had with him, in cash, about two hundred guilders, the hard savings of a ten years' military servitude. With the whole of this sum he bribed three of the sailors,– such was the sacrifice he was prepared to make . . .

"At day-break, one exceedingly fine, calm morning, he and his three companions left the vessel, clandestinely, in one of the ship's boats. His friends hoped to be back the same evening, and trusted to assuage the captain's wrath with some plausible story, accounting for their day's absence. The distance they had to row was about five miles; and the day remaining true to its fair promise at dawn, the party thought they had every prospect of effecting a safe landing.

"Nothing marked their progress until they had nearly reached the outermost roller, when they lay on their oars for awhile, anxiously watching the dashing of the surf ahead of them. The prospect was certainly formidable, for the rollers, three in number, advanced in shore in rapid succession, breaking about two hundred yards from the beach, and surging over it with a roar plainly audible to our adventuring friends in the boat, who now felt their courage sinking fast. They would even then have abandoned their attempt, and returned to the ship, had it not been for the persuasion and entreaty of Van Bengel, who, blinded to the realities of the dangers before them, would have risked anything rather than relinquish his project, and with it his hopes, now so soon to be consummated. Encouraged at last by his arguments, and the golden prospects he held out to them, besides the reality of the two hundred guilders, they prepared for carrying out their rash attempt; and waiting for a momentary smooth, pulled in with the outer roller, which, however, soon outstripped them. They were now in the midst of it, and to turn back was too late, for another swell had already started onwards in their wake. With throbbing hearts, and eyes eagerly strained on the fast-approaching surge, they pulled with the mad vigour of those who too well dreaded the gigantic wave that would soon overtake them. It came. A steer-oar might have maintained the boat's direction, and thus have lessened the shock; but their now unmanageable rudder left them no alternative but to meet the full force of the coming roller "broadside on" . . . The boat was swamped, and thrown keel upwards; and while his companions were swept away, Van Bengel succeeded in clinging to it. Thus buoyed up, he drifted to the shore, which was only a few hundred yards distant, and which he soon reached, in certainly no enviable plight, but not a little delighted at his very narrow escape.

"We shall not follow Van Bengel in his wanderings on shore. Suffice it to say that he at last reached the spot where, as he fully believed, the treasure lay hidden. He had clambered up to the cleft in the rock, from which the fresh water rill was gushing forth, with all the mock impetuosity of a miniature cascade; and to his inexpressible joy he also found exactly as it had been described to him, another narrow but apparently deep opening in the rock, close by. Creeping in as well as he could, he was soon able to stand upright. He had evidently set foot in some vast grotto, but the only light entering it being from the narrow opening through which he had come, only a very small portion of the cave within a few feet from him was visible. He eagerly groped for the expected money-bags, but nothing more valuable than a rusty cutlass and a stockless old Dutch blunderbuss rewarded his search. He now became more eager for a light, and recollecting that he had a small burning-glass in his pocket, he succeeded, after emerging again from the grotto, in kindling a fire on the beach, and having collected some dry pieces of ship's timber, which he found in abundance, he was soon able, after a few trips for a sufficiency of fuel, to illuminate a large portion of the grotto by a roaring fire inside. More old weapons he now discovered lying strewn about. But, alas, he found no treasure yet. The streamlet which issued from the cleft meandered nearly through the middle of the cave, which rose in height and increased in width the further he penetrated, until at last deepening darkness rendered exploration impracticable. He searched and searched again, but in vain. With the aid of a cutlass he dug about, wherever he thought money might possibly be buried, until at last, in despair and utterly exhausted, he retraced his steps past the fire, which was now waning fast, to the mouth of the cave; when he found to his astonishment that the sun had already set, and to his horror that the tide was up, and that egress was then impossible. Nothing therefore was left for him but to remain where he was till next morning. He now bethought himself of some biscuits, and a well-filled stone jar of Schiedam, which had washed on shore with the shattered boat, to which it had been secured in a bag and which he had taken into the cave, but in his intense activity had hitherto forgotten. The little hunger he felt was soon appeased with his frugal fare, and perhaps for this reason, as also in order to alleviate the despondency which, with his extreme lassitude, brooded over him more deeply, he felt the inspiring draughts he took more welcome than his ordinary sober habits might otherwise have made them. Having selected the least uncomfortable nook for a resting-place, he hoped soon in sleep to forget, for some time at least, his misery. But bitter thoughts of his failure—of his recent career—of the friends whom he had lost and forsaken—and of his own wretched solitariness, crowded on his mind in all the phantasy of an over-wrought and now re-acting imagination. Several hours, he thought, were spent by him in this melancholy reverie, when of a sudden the embers of the fire which he had lit, and had watched dying-out to the last spark,—as if by magic, blazed up with almost the effulgence of the sun itself. The whole grotto was illumined with the brightness of day, to its innermost recesses; and before Gert van Bengel had recovered from his astonishment, a large number of figures, dressed in sailors' apparel,—but the latter, of such grotesqueness and huge proportions as could only have been worn by a bygone century—seemed to issue from the back of the cave, and approach the fire, round which they soon completed a circle. With a heavy measured tramp they danced, or rather trudged, round the now high-flaming faggots, with grizzly beards, elongated visages, fantastically shaped hats, and broad belts encircling their loose hanging costume; while some wore large sheathed knives, and others antique-looking swords dangling from their sides. About a dozen rounds had been completed, when one of them, happening to take a step backwards, upset Van Bengel's stone bottle, but immediately picked it up again, and applied it to his mouth with the eagerness of an old connoisseur who had long been debarred from enjoying anything so good. In fact, when he removed the jar from his lips, it was empty; but as if to make up for his lagging behind–for the rest had gone on without him–he cut such odd capers in the air as brought his circle of companions to a stand-still, as if in perfect surprise.

"A number of others, of similar appearance and provided with old-fashioned triangular spades and other implements, now also entered from the back of the cave, and at about the centre of it soon diverted a portion of the rivulet, for about a dozen paces, into a somewhat semi-circular trench which they had previously cut, and thereupon digging into the waterless portion of the bed, brought up from the bottom at least a dozen massive iron money-chests, to each of which the fellow who had smacked Van Bengel's Schiedam applied a ponderous key: at the same time wide opening each chest as he passed along. The whole of the circle around the fire had by this time joined the additional party.

"Gert van Bengel, who through fear of being discovered, had hitherto kept himself in the back-ground as much as possible, could now no longer restrain himself from seeing with his own eyes the extent of the treasure in the chests. Judging wisely, that without approaching, he would be able sufficiently to secure his purpose by a more elevated position, he was preparing himself for his "bird's eye view" by placing his foot on a projecting stone above him,–when unfortunately it gave way, and losing his balance, he tumbled on the sloping ground below, and rolled right into the midst of the assemblage. Opening his eyes, while still on all fours, he could just see the figures rush off, as if panic-struck, towards the back of the cave, for in an instant all was dark!

"To be pursued by a ghost may well be supposed to unnerve the stoutest heart, but when the tables are turned, and not only a solitary spectre, but a whole regiment of them, scamper away from us in promiscuous flight, our courage may be presumed to rise, on the other hand, in equal proportion. We need not, therefore, be surprised that Gert van Bengel, after having in vain felt for the money-chests, which he thought they had left behind, also followed. All, however, was pitch dark.

"Having groped his way for some distance, he joyfully perceived a beam of the moon, which he knew was full at the time, falling through an opening in the grotto overhead.

"He had soon clambered up to this outlet, and peering through it from his new position, he could distinctly see again his strange visitors to the cave (whose numbers now appeared to have increased considerably) busily engaged in burying afresh their immense money-chests beneath the vast sandheaps at the back of the cliff, and which he had already visited the day before. Although watching them at some distance, he was still fully able to observe all their movements, for the moon was shining in all its brightness, and the snowwhite sandmasses as a background made their dark figures stand out in bold and clear relief.

"Having sufficiently satisfied his curiosity, and carefully noted the spots where the chests were buried, Van Bengel retraced his steps into the cave as well as the darkness would permit him.

"Gert van Bengel awoke next morning with a splitting headache, and it was some time before he could consecutively recollect the marvellous events of the night. His remembrance of his tumble, which had so untowardly broken the spell of the midnight meeting, clearly explained the pains he felt in his head. It however puzzled him not a little to find that he was still occupying about the same spot in the grotto where he had originally lain down. He could only ascribe it to some extraordinary but yet possible chance, by which he had found his way back, while groping in the dark, to the exact nook he had come from. If, however, a shadow of doubt still flittered across Gert van Bengel's mind, as to the reality of what he now remembered–here was a perfect "crucial instance"–a broad palpable fact not to be gainsaid: *his stone bottle, which he recollected having left more than half full, lay perfectly empty at some distance from him.* Not a drop in it was left: to such a degree had that galligaskined caperer relished the pilfered sample from the jolly Dutch captain's bin.

"With new blown hopes, Van Bengel now prepared to leave his dark retreat, for the sandhills–the fondly pictured scene of his future labours. The tide being down, he had no difficulty in again reaching the beach, and was soon engaged in levelling, with a broad flat piece of iron he had picked up, a sand-mound which he thought he identified as one of the number, where, from his watching place, he had seen that the treasure was buried. The height, however, was more than 200 feet. Several days' hard work would therefore be necessary to enable him to gain his object. He laboured the whole day, and returned early the next morning to continue with new vigour. But on coming to the spot again, he found, to his astonishment, that every vestige of his previous day's exertions had disappeared. The very iron, several feet long, and which he had left standing on end where he had ceased to work, was gone; and moreover the whole aspect of the hills appeared changed from what it was the previous day. He felt puzzled. He now selected what he thought was another treasure-hill, but of smaller dimensions. Here he dug till the evening, leaving his levelling iron on end on the surface as before; but alas! when he returned the following morning, he again found, to his mortification, that no trace of his labours was left. Thus Gert van Bengel toiled on for several days more, with ever-tantalised but fast dwindling hopes; until at last the conviction which had strongly dawned on him became perfect in his mind, that his mysterious visitors in the cave were the secret counterworkers of all his attempts–by restoring in the night his demolishing work of the day, and at the same time varying surrounding appearances in order still better to mislead his search!

"A few days more saw Gert van Bengel, with now totally crushed hopes, a solitary wanderer along the coast, with the perilous object of reaching Cape Town overland ...

"On his arrival in Cape Town [[after a four months' journey]], Gert van Bengel at once repaired to the Castle with the chimerical hope of inducing the Governor to send out a ship to excavate the treasure at the sandhills, but Father Tulbagh's practical and disciplinarian mind decided upon issuing an order for the *ci-devant* corporal's immediate "deportation" to Holland instead. On the home voyage, Van Bengel employed himself in writing an account of his adventures. Shortly after his landing at Helvoetsluys, it was found that his mind had given way, and he was placed in an asylum, where he ultimately died ...

"At this very day [[the article concludes]], the traveller in Olifant's Hoek may now and then meet with some "old boer," who shakes his time-worn pate mysteriously when speaking of the shifting sands on the coast, calling them the "Devil's mole-hills;" and may listen to marvellous tales of immense sums of money lying buried at Woody Cape. There is also a tradition current amongst the farmers, that one of their progenitors, one morning, discovered at the beach below the cliff a large iron ring which the waves had washed bare, and which evidently belonged to some huge iron chest, too heavy for him to lift; that he brought his span of oxen to the spot to drag out the treasure, when, just as they were moving away with it, the tide rushed in, and farmer, oxen, and all, were swept away into the ocean and never heard of again. This, it is said, is the reason why, amongst the farmers there, Woody Cape has hitherto borne the ominous name of Kwaai Hoek [[Angry Corner]].

It is easy to dismiss van Bengel's story as the rantings of an unstable mind. In David Allen's view however there are good reasons for accepting that it has a basis in truth. It is important to notice at once that the *Dodington* survivor who told van Bengel of the treasure did not say, or even suggest, that it was from his own ship. There is therefore no suggestion of a clandestine voyage to the mainland by Jones and his brother officers to hide the treasure. In fact the survivor went so far as to say that Jones buried the *Dodington* treasure on the island.

David's attitude to van Bengel's story is based on a detailed examination of the journals of the survivors and of the 1757 newspaper report. In both Jones said there were clear signs of previous shipwrecks on the island. Indeed in the *Public Advertiser* he went so far as to identify one of these as probably Dutch and the other English. While he said that signs of camps were found, with evidence that the previous survivors had also built some sort of boat, he does not mention finding graves or skeletons. The clear assumption must be that earlier survivors were able to build some sort of vessel and sail to the mainland. David believes that having landed near Woody Cape, and being fearful of attack from the Africans, previous survivors would seek first to hide their valuables where they could be found again easily. What more convenient place could there be than a cave almost concealed by a fresh water stream? He argues further that the *Dodington* men, subject to more or less the same amount of drift as they crossed from the island, would land somewhere near the stream. Then, after such a long haul, and perhaps influenced by the shock of losing a friend in the surf, they would go in search of water; and that when they came across the conspicuous stream they found both cave and treasure.

Chapter 8

More scientific efforts than that of Gert van Bengel to find the *Dodington* have been frustrated by a number of factors. The first is that both the survivors and the navigators of *HMS Stag* incorrectly pin-pointed the rock they thought the ship must have struck. The second is that the island is a repository for wrecks in Algoa Bay. The current which scours round the inner limits of the Bay takes with it any vessel not wholly under control and drops it there. A third and simpler factor is that the island is so difficult to see and was in the past so inaccurately charted. For the second reason in particular, any artefact found on Bird Island has been assumed to be from the *Dodington*, whereas the survivors of that wreck made it clear that other shipwreck victims had camped there before, and that the island was already strewn with wreckage when they arrived. What is certain is that a large anchor which has been conspicuous on the south-east side of the island ever since the wreck, and which has been photographed since the mid-nineteenth century, did come from the *Dodington*. It was recently moved from its resting place by a helicopter crew who deposited it near the present lighthouse some hundreds of yards away.

One earlier report of *Dodington* artefacts being taken from the island was made in 1824, when the harbour master of what is now known as Port Alfred, John Dyason, sailed to the island in a lifeboat and returned with copper gun ladles. These were used for pouring powder into cannon, and he believed that they must have come from the ship.

In 1850 there were newspaper reports that an early guano ship had "brought up wreckage from the *Dodington*". The story is interesting, but incorrect. The tale involves the brig *Norfolk*, owned by an early Port Elizabeth entrepreneur and shipping magnate, John Owen Smith, an Englishman with a flair for making money from what others often regarded as hare-brained business propositions. He had the concession for guano on the island, and used the *Norfolk* for shipping it. In 1850 she was moving from one side of the island to the other when the wind fell and she struck Seal Island. *Norfolk* was got off the island, but so badly damaged that she was deliberately steered back on to the rocks. In a later report the *Eastern Province Telegraph* wrote that the *Norfolk* had previously "brought up 24 pounder brass cannon; iron bolts; and the shank and flukes of an anchor" from the *Dodington*. The cannon were in fact of iron; besides which, the *Dodington* did not carry brass guns. The gun is now in the grounds of the oceanarium at the Port Elizabeth museum.

The major problem for anyone setting out to look for the *Dodington* is the confusion between the rock the survivors thought the ship struck, and that which those on the *Stag*, in cavalier fashion, later named Dodington Rock. The reefs on the south-east side of the island were named West Reef, South Reef and Dodington Rock by the *Stag* staff. Looking at it this way, the survivors' accounts make it clear that they believed the ship had struck East Rock, the farthest east. (As a result of later observations the order in which the reefs were named was changed on the charts so that they became West Reef, Dodington Rock and East Reef.)

The confusion is easily explained. West Reef and what is now Dodington Rock are almost always clearly visible; East Reef is submerged, and shows on the surface only as a breaking patch of water. The worthy gentlemen of *HMS Stag*, no doubt seeing a rock above water in about the same place where the *Dodington* might have been believed to strike, therefore named it Dodington Rock.

To find the *Dodington* a completely fresh look at the area was required, and any idea that she was on or near Dodington Rock put out of mind. During his school days David Allen, whose discovery of the *Dodington* will be described in the following pages, frequently went on what were necessarily abortive expeditions with the Port Elizabeth Subaqua Diving Club to search for the *Dodington*. His interest aroused, he spasmodically pursued the search over the next ten years, at times forgetting about the ship for long periods, at times working hard at finding her. Most often he and diving friends would launch ski boats from Woody Cape to go across to the island, but like the luckless survivors of the wreck they usually found themselves spending more time righting their boats in the surf than diving.

Then came a lucky stroke of fortune when David, on national service in the South African Navy in 1970, was able to spend considerable time anchored off the island aboard the frigate *SAS President Kruger*. At times he found himself wincing at the uncanny similarity between his circumstances and those of Gert van Bengel who had also found himself ship-bound there, although the *President Kruger* was not under repair. But without going underwater, David was able to study the wave action, collate distances, and take useful colour pictures of the area both from the deck and, when flying in the ship's helicopter, from the air. His conclusion was the same as that reached many years earlier by Sir Richard Temple, that the ship had certainly not struck Dodington Rock.

"In the first place" as David later pointed out "it was obvious that if the ship went 'all to pieces' in twenty minutes after striking, she could never have covered the mile and a half between Dodington Rock, or even what is now East Reef, and the island. The very heavy anchor washed ashore shows that she must have struck close in. There is further evidence for this. Webb said in his account that he had been washed ashore 'on a plank with a nail in my shoulder'. I don't think he could have made it from that distance away under such a handicap, especially as he would have been swept away by the currents. The survivors also appear to have been washed ashore comparatively closely grouped. It is unlikely that this would have been the case if they were being washed in from afar. Then again, so much came ashore from the wreck, which would have been washed far out to sea had it been scattered by the waves a mile and a half from shore.

"In all the story seemed arrant nonsense. I believe that Jones and Webb deliberately gave incorrect information in the hope that Comany treasure could eventually be salvaged. What remained was to pinpoint where the ship really lay."

Having left the Navy, David returned home. Between working for a tyre company, routine dives with the South African police reserve squad, and his other day-to-day activities, he sporadically pursued the search for the *Dodington*. His efforts concentrated more and more on library researches, in which he was helped by the ever-enthusiastic Alf Porter, chief librarian at Port Elizabeth's public library. His researches led him to believe that the ship was even closer inshore than he had first imagined. He went back time and again to study his slides and pictures, watching in particular for the wave action on the south-east corner of the island. There were good reasons for looking for the wreck in that area. First Sir Richard Temple had said that the lights on the first lighthouse, when lined up, would point to the wreck site. Then there was the anchor lying on the rocks below the lighthouse but just a little removed from it. David became convinced from his observations that there was an inshore reef on which the ship had struck; but one so close to the island that many people assumed that the waves which broke on it were breaking on the outer rim of the island itself.

His enthusiasm to find the ship increased appreciably after he had teamed up with university student Gerry van Niekerk, a learner diver of his own age whose passion to explore underwater matched his own. Together they slowly broke away from the regular diving clubs, spear fishing, and other more placid forms of diving, to search the Port Elizabeth coast for wrecks. Their efforts were soon concentrated on one wreck in particular, the Portuguese galleon *Sacramento*,

Clockwise: (TL) Gerry van Niekerk cleaning the 12-pounder.
(TR) a howitzer before cleaning
(LR) some of the twenty tons of copper salvaged; the bun shaped ingots were known as barbary heads
(LL) after 222 years the 12-pounder proved to be in perfect condition – George II's monogram.

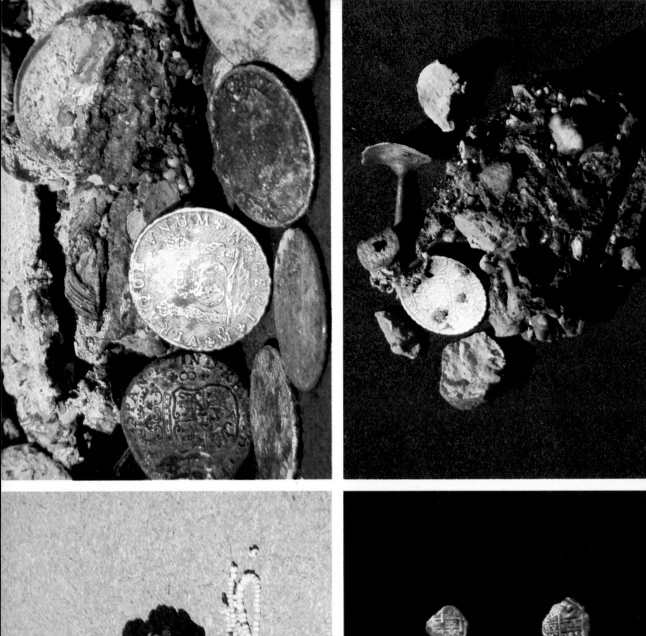

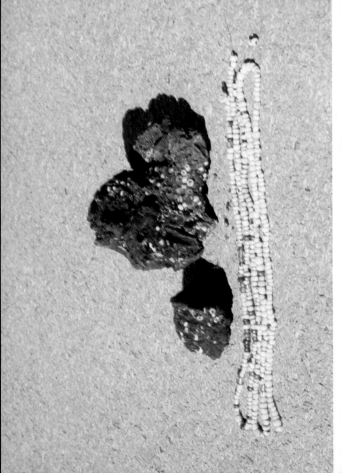

which with her huge strategic cargo of new founded cannon from Macao sank somewhere near Port Elizabeth on her maiden voyage to Portugal in 1647. The story of how they discovered the *Sacramento* and recovered forty magnificent bronze cannon is told in a companion volume; what were common to both expeditions were the problems ashore which bedevilled the work of salvage.

In April 1977, a rival team of divers, who had paid R2,500 for the exact location of the *Sacramento* cannon, arrived from Cape Town with a boat and equipment intending to conduct their own salvage on the site on the basis of every man for himself. Working rapidly ashore, David managed to contract them into his own salvage team on the basis that they would have a share in the cannon not yet lifted. It was, he believed, the only way of preventing an ugly, and potentially fatal, encounter on the dangerous site where, with four tons of cannon being lifted right in the surf, a man could be killed through the slightest slip. It proved expensive. David has reckoned that in all the manoeuvre cost his team R22,500.

Diffficulties also developed with the Port Elizabeth Museum which are reflected in the published statements of its director Dr John Wallace and historian Mrs Dee Nash. Shortly after the *Sacramento* discovery David called a meeting of interested historical bodies, including the museum, in order that the wreck could be properly researched and the finds noted. In a press report after the meeting of April 2, 1977, Dr Wallace said, "I and my staff have studied the cannon and are satisfied that their recovery has been conducted in a businesslike and highly responsible manner . . . The salvage team have done a fine job and have acted most responsibly. They have also done a great deal of research." Then again on June 10, 1977, Dr Wallace told another newspaper, "Mr Allen who has been working in close collaboration with the museum, will continue to do so as its nautical archaeology associate."

By May 1978, however, Mrs Nash told a public meeting in Port Elizabeth that the divers had been "incompetent" and that the wreck would have been better left untouched until "some proper authority" could have worked the site. Her complaint was that the site had not been laid out in accordance with normal archaeological digs, as she claimed other underwater sites had been. Her speech left David seething, while his lawyer scanned it for libel. (And apart from the other matters in her speech, the suggestion that an underwater site could be laid out in pounding surf with only a few diving days a month at best is a curious one.) In July 1978 Dr Wallace also told a Port Elizabeth newspaper, " . . . instead of going in and dragging the cannon off the site it would be better to study the wood construction at the site . . . Salvors and fortune hunters can wreck an historical shipwreck and a law is urgently needed in South Africa to protect wreck sites from exploitation and make them subject to the same rules as archaeological digs". (Again it may be pointed out that only one piece of ship's timbers was found on the *Sacramento* site, that its position in relation to the shore was noted, and that the wood itself was brought ashore for examination.) Such were the difficulties which David and Gerry faced ashore, and which caused them to avoid conducting their researches into the *Dodington* as openly as they had done in the case of the *Sacramento*.

But to return to May 1977. It was in this month, towards the end of the *Sacramento* project, that David and Gerry turned their attention to the *Dodington*, confident that if they could keep the project a secret and properly under control, they could salvage the ship without the difficulties which hampered their previous effort.

They therefore cast about for a discreet trawler skipper and crew to undertake the effort, and tried to decide on an adequate "cover story" to explain why they were spending long spells on Bird Island; for by now they were being watched, virtually night and day, by the local Press as well as by a Cape Town diving team in Port Elizabeth.

Treasure clockwise: (TL) glass beads; strung and in the conglomerate form in which most of the artefacts were found; four barrels of these were taken on board for trading.

(TR) Pieces of eight in conglomerate; encrustment was well advanced in two centuries, making sea-bed detection difficult.

(LL) Pieces of eight, of four and of two: the 'pillar dollar' insignia on the reverse became the basis of the American $ sign.

(LR) Conglomerate with red lead paint, lead weights and silver coin.

Chapter 9

In the closing fortnight of the *Sacramento* adventure David and Gerry got the opportunity they needed to begin the search for the *Dodington*. A friend told David that the Atlas Fertiliser Company, which owned the guano concession on Bird Island, wanted someone to carry out a feasibility survey before deciding whether or not to build a new jetty on the island. David made inquiries and found that Atlas held a ten year guano concession from the South African Government Department of Sea Fisheries; and that in addition to the survey they also needed a boat to ferry convict workmen out to the island and bring back the guano. "What could have been more ideal?" David commented later. "We could use the trawler we had hired for the *Sacramento* job for collecting guano, and give ourselves perfect cover for being on the island. The trawler would, of course, ferry back by night anything we found on the island." David phoned Atlas and spoke to the managing director (and freelance journalist) René Lion-Cachet, who agreed that in return for surveying the jetty free of charge, David and his team would live free in one of the houses used on the island by the guano collectors. He arranged to fly to Port Elizabeth for further talks and a trip out to the island.

At four o'clock on a cold and squally morning, David, Gerry, and René boarded the trawler *Etosha* for their voyage to the island, thirty-six miles away across the storm tossed Algoa Bay. The old trawler groaned and rose in a lurch to port as she gathered speed past the Port Elizabeth harbour signal station and broke the lee of the breakwater in a pre-dawn not yet brightened by the cloud-filtered sun.

Skipper George Braxton swung the wheel as *Etosha* sank broadside into the trough of the wave, and opened the throttles to make her turn faster so that she rose on the succeeding wave at near right angles, a manoeuvre which sent the bows crashing down into the following trough. Spray shot up against the bridge, clattering on the windows as the coloured crew huddled in the stern brewing coffee. In the signal station a lonely duty officer paused to watch the trawler turn out of sight behind the breakwater; and then went into the warmth of his office high above the harbour wall to enter her departure time and destination.

Etosha is a sturdy, shallow draught West Coast trawler built when the fishing industry of Namibia was at its boom peak before the Russian, Japanese and industrialised South African fishing companies killed the fish in their millions and cleaned out the hunting grounds. A single-propeller boat with one slow but reliable engine, *Etosha* had seen a moment of fleeting glory as the "star" of a film about the fishing industry called *Wild Seasons*. Later she had been lengthened to eighty feet to increase her capacity to sixty tons, and with ample space for fuel and food below decks could remain at sea comfortably for ten days at a stretch. She had been based in Port Elizabeth for several years after a local man, Gert Botha, bought her. She also had adequate lifting gear to pick up almost anything the *Dodington* was likely to give up.

David and Gerry had hired the *Etosha* to lift the *Sacramento* guns, and found her ideal for the purpose. They also got along well with skipper George Braxton. At twenty-five, both of them unable to conceal their delight not only at what lay ahead, but at what they had recently achieved, they stood in the wheelhouse with George and René shivering in the morning cold.

That day however little was done on the island – the sea was too rough to allow the plastic guano bags in *Etosha's* hold to be unloaded or to allow a party to land. David and Gerry however returned to Port Elizabeth with a firm understanding between themselves and René.

Three days later *Etosha* sailed again for the island. Aboard with David and Gerry this time was a learner diver, Dave Smale, who was soon to find himself thrown in at the deep end of top class salvage work. Dave had an excellent knowledge of the surf, having been a keen surf board rider for years. David and Gerry felt his experience would be valuable in the conditions they expected to encounter on the *Dodington* site, especially as they intended that "Little Dave" would be left in charge of their motorised rubber dinghy while they dived.

With better weather than on the previous trip the party were able to land on the island. They decided that as the guano bags were made of plastic there would be no harm in floating them across to the landing stage from the trawler, and so with a party of men on either side and ropes attached to each load the job was quickly accomplished. The *Etosha* then returned to Port Elizabeth where David and Gerry hastily completed work on the *Sacramento*. On May 20, 1977, they were therefore able to declare work on the Portuguese ship finished, and turned their whole attention to the work still to come on the *Dodington*.

Bird Island is an extraordinary and somewhat eerie place. So near the major industrial city of Port Elizabeth, it is nonetheless so utterly isolated that few people go near it apart from convicts sent to load guano, and railway officials who service the now automated lighthouse once a month. Sometimes parties of naturalists venture there, but in recent years they too have tended to ignore the island.

What makes Bird Island doubly dangerous are the huge swells which run in any weather, and the ring of death formed by the large Great White Death Shark population. As an example of ecological balance Bird Island is probably a classic. The sharks which cordon the island, and which live only to kill, feed on the Cape fur seals and penguins. These tend to stick together on the smaller island known as Black Rock for some measure of protection, but go in daily search of the huge fish population, thus making themselves easy prey for the sharks. The fish are so abundant that at times divers cannot see more than a few feet in front of them as the water becomes alive with darting shoals. Yet while the seals feed on the fish and in turn become prey to the sharks, the balance appears to remain more or less equal, and probably has since before the wreck of the *Dodington*.

Apart from the new lighthouse there are several buildings on the island, including two old houses once used by the lighthousemen but now deserted. The wife of a former lighthouseman is said to haunt the island and her ghost clatters about the house at night – or so the legend goes. At a decent distance from the houses is a row of rude graves where lighthousemen who died on service are buried. These shallow graves, marked with small crosses and heaped with white stones, serve to remind the visitor of the aura of death which hangs over the island and has haunted it since first civilised man named it Chaos Island. On the far side of the island are three other houses and a large guano storage shed, as well as the jetty from which guano is ferried to waiting ships or trawlers. Several paths criss-cross the island, all neatly signposted by lines of whitewashed stones. Perhaps this very appearance of orderliness, both in nature and in the evidence of man's occupation, increases the shiver which runs down the spine of the visitor who realises how death lurks just below the surface of the sea and how dreadful has been the fate of so many seamen on these jagged shores. There have been some ten shipwrecks around the island, each with its large contingent of dead.

Then, too, there are the birds. Around the foot of the lighthouse, and usually covering an area several hundred yards square, the gannets gather in their hundreds of thousands. Their constant movement, and the noise produced by the ceaseless flapping of their wings, heighten the bizarre atmosphere. When a dozen or more birds rise into the air their places are immediately filled – sometimes, it seems, by birds conjured from the air. As one arrives on the island by helicopter it almost seems as if the island is alive as the birds jostle one another, coming and going all the time with no apparent purpose but to change places in the flock.

Three men live on the island. The "Headman" is Oom Piet Oodendaal – Oom, an Afrikaaner word meaning "uncle", is a term of endearment and respect used of any one irrespective of relationship. Oom Piet, who is employed by the South African Department of Sea Fisheries to ensure that no one lands on the island without authority and to see that the birds are not unduly disturbed, also maintains the buildings and equipment and manages the collection, storage, and shipment of the guano. He keeps in touch with the mainland through radio equipment in the lighthouse. He reports daily when the light comes on, and more urgently if it does not. He is a taciturn man who speaks only when it suits him, and when he does it is largely about his war exploits. What he did between being demobbed and taking up his job on the island remains his secret, but from time to time he would play a tune on his old concertina and tell of his adventures during the war. Often, particularly when the weather was bad, he retired to bed at 4.30 pm to read a book from his extensive collection. At times he would fish, but more frequently he would listen to the daily radio serials and wait patiently for the call from shore to check that the lighthouse was functioning.

With Oom Piet is the official island cook, Kallie Swartland, whose culinary gifts are prodigious, especially with seafoods. He is one of a family of fifteen, and has been in the Sea Fisheries "island service" for some years since he left his employment in diamond dredging barges off the Namibian coast. While on the island he is abstinent, but his visits to Cape Town on leave are a different matter. While David and Gerry were on the island Kallie spent three weeks excitedly telling them what he planned to do during his leave; then, dapperly dressed in suit and hat, he flew off in a helicopter on the first leg to Cape Town. When he came back three weeks later – it was his first break in almost three years – he was subdued for a fortnight and hardly spoke at all. When he broke his silence it was to say that he had finally recovered from the hangover he got in Cape Town. Kallie has only been on Bird Island since early 1974, which makes him a new comer both to Oom Piet and to the oldest inhabitant, an African known only as Jack.

Over six feet tall, and appearing almost as wide, Jack can turn his hand to any odd job on the island. He can carry out complex repairs to boats and equipment with only the most rudimentary tools. His knowledge of the guano cycle and its collection is encyclopaedic, and without him much of the work would not be done. Among his possessions he has some of the finest fishing gear available, including an excellent array of shark hooks and specialised fishing gear, most of it gleaned from departing lighthouse men, and all of it lovingly maintained. He is unusually competent with the handling of the island longboat – which is peculiar for an African, whose tribal instincts normally dictate that the sea is best left alone – and in a tough spot in rough weather, Jack is the man to have in command of the longboat.

As the *Dodington* survivors noted, the island is peculiarly healthy, partly no doubt as a result of the ammonia fumes which rise from the guano; and Jack in common with Oom Piet and Kallie enjoys excellent health.

Late in May 1977 David, Gerry van Niekerk and "Little Dave" Smale installed themselves in the house on the island designated for the holder of the guano concession. The house, sparsely furnished, having no beds and lit only by gas lamps, had three bedrooms, a bathroom and kitchen with gas cooker, so there was at least space for the men to make themselves comfortable. While David and Gerry assembled beds from wooden boards and covered them with sleeping bags, and arranged lamps for each room, Little Dave took charge of his favourite quarters in any house – the kitchen. Though slightly built he has an amazing appetite, and sheer necessity has obliged him to become an excellent cook, a fact which David and Gerry turned to good account throughout their five months stay on the island. "There were times when we were really despondent and felt like giving it all up as we walked back to the house – only to smell from yards off Little Dave's cooking, and then, after a wash and a hearty meal, the world seemed wonderfully benign again. I reckon we owe Little Dave quite a lot for making sure that as far as the inner man went we were as comfortable as we could be out there," Gerry said.

On that first day ashore, the plastic bags from *Etosha* safely stored, David and Gerry sat down to take stock of the position. Their first concern was that of safety. Both knew that below the surface of the sea the sharks swam tirelessly in search of food, killing indiscriminately for the sake of killing. In the past they had seen big seals float by with their heads and half their bodies missing after one huge bite from a Great White shark. Even before Hollywood glamorised

Great Whites in the film *Jaws*, their potential killing power was well known to any South African with the vaguest interest in the sea. Too often bathers, particularly near Durban, were mutilated by sharks swimming in search of food near the river mouths. To dive off Bird Island was inviting attack, and no such encounter would ever leave a diver a whole man. Indeed the secrets of the island reefs remained intact so long because few men dared venture into those waters for fear of being bitten by a shark. But David and Gerry knew that provided they exercised extreme caution they would be safe enough.

Once under water their only real weapon was their "shark banger". A shark banger consists of a three-foot-long metal rod with a twelve-gauge shot gun cartridge at the end. To use it effectively the diver must swim to within three feet of the shark's gaping jaws and then ram the explosive end of the banger against the sensitive skin of the animal. The banger has a firing pin exactly like a gun, and when this is activated by the thrust of the stick against the shark's body the cartridge explodes. The percussion either stuns or kills the shark depending on how accurate the blow has been, the best shot being at the shark's extremely sensitive nose. "But if you miss you are right where you should never venture, at the front end of an enraged shark. Once they are roused, Great Whites will attack everything and anything. Their whole bodies are one huge killing muscle and they can move like lightning," Gerry comments. But like David, he would rather be underwater armed with a banger than swimming on the surface, not knowing whether a shark was coming up at him from below or not.

What David and Gerry did not foresee was that the wreck of the *Dodington* had become the territorial area of a giant fifteen foot Great White who came to be christened Alfred, and who was to cause them several scares over the following weeks. From their previous encounters with sharks David and Gerry had found that if a shark came too close for comfort it was safest to swim straight at it. "This tended to frighten sharks away, not because they are cowardly creatures, but probably because they needed to assess the situation and plan another attack. Whatever the reason we had found that by doing this and using the shark bangers judiciously we had never been attacked, although we had some very nasty experiences," David said.

They also decided not to use their usual method of searching for wrecks, which is to be towed behind a motor-powered rubber dinghy so that maximum ground area can be covered in a short time. "The trouble is that a diver in a black wet suit looks awfully like a seal swimming on the surface, and neither of us felt like being a human fishing fly," said Gerry.

Having decided that Little Dave would only be allowed to do a few shallow depth snorkel dives at first while he learnt the ropes, and that for most of the time he would remain in the dinghy keeping a sharp eye out for sharks or any other intruder, David and Gerry set off round the island to inspect what was to become their home.

One curious incident had taken place some time before when they first came out to the island with René Lion-Cachet. David had stared from the wheelhouse of *Etosha* in amazement when he saw a highly coloured rainbow hanging over the island, its end pointing exactly to the spot where he expected to find the *Dodington*. Whispering his surprise to Gerry, he went out on deck with a camera to photograph this strange phenomenon. As Gerry joined him David confided, "That's where the *Dodington* is". Gerry still confesses to being sceptical of such a pronouncement, and to wondering whether David was on this occasion pulling his leg.

It was with quickening hearts that they approached the side of the island in the shadow of the lighthouse, for it was off this coast that they expected to find the wreck. They knew from their library researches that a great fluked anchor lay on the rocks below high water mark, and felt confident that this was an anchor from the *Dodington*. (The anchor was later moved by helicopter to a point on shore nearer the lighthouse. The reason for this move, and who ordered it, are uncertain, but the chief marker to the *Dodington* site has therefore been effectively removed.) On this and subsequent searches along the shore they found not only the anchor, which was readily visible, but bits of bottle, shards of old pottery, a piece of lead and a thin piece of copper sheeting, together with some conglomerates of sand and sealife containing iron as well. It seemed a fair bet that these had been washed ashore from the wreck, and that the

Dodington lay under the sea not far from where they stood. The men returned to the house for supper and made their plans.

The plastic guano bags in *Etosha* had been unloaded, the food for David's party was safely ashore and skipper George Braxton intended sailing late the next day for Port Elizabeth, his work for the meantime finished. David and Gerry had little hope that the weather would be suitable for diving on the *Dodington* next day because they had that night seen a substantial swell over what they assumed to be the site. However May 29 dawned bright and calm, with the sea as smooth as it ever is around the island and hardly a breath of wind. After lunch, the morning having been spent in preparations which included some last minute dashes to *Etosha* to ensure that nothing had been left behind, the trio launched the rubber dinghy, and with racing pulses opened the throttle of the outboard motor to move round to the south-east side of the island.

David piloted the dinghy into position over the reef where he expected to find the ship. His first concern once he had anchored was that the current ran much faster than he had calculated, and that this would make diving so close inshore even more hazardous. He decided however that they should make an exploratory dive. Gerry donned his snorkel to conduct a fast search over the whole of the area, while David strapped an aqualung to his back intending to make a search of the bottom. In this way they would have fairly comprehensive coverage on their first attempt.

David and Gerry slipped off the dinghy, their shark bangers securely tied to their wrists. David Smale grinned a cheerful "Good Luck" and waved as the men dipped below the sea. For some minutes they swam independently. Let the next developments be given in David's own words. "Once underwater I started going over in my mind the knowledge gained from my years of research on the *Dodington*. I had a strange confidence that she must be somewhere beneath me. It was exactly 222 years since she was wrecked and I was determined to find her. After I had been underwater only a few minutes I suddenly looked down and knew that those ten years of research had paid off.

"It is very hard to explain the thrill of first seeing such a sight. Below me, about twenty feet deep, lay a huge mound of what appeared to be about twenty tons of copper ingots. On top of that lay the ship's bow anchor, a huge fluked anchor perhaps twelve feet in length. Sticking out of that mountain of dull green copper were cannons, silenced for two centuries, and now the homes of small fish and octopuses which flitted in and out of the barrels. At a glance I could see all around bits and pieces of wreckage and cargo. On the upper side of the mound was a perfect bronze cannon six feet in length encrusted with white coral. Lying on one side, on a bed of neat, round stones, lay a green patinated brass carronade about three feet long. Later we were to find two more of these carronades, or 'murderers' as they were called by the men who used them. First made at Carron in Scotland, they were given their nickname because they were brought into use only when two ships lay locked together. Short, stubby, wide-mouthed guns, they were used to spray the decks and rigging of the enemy with pounds of round lead balls very much like large modern shotgun ammunition. This grapeshot would fan out across the deck, knocking down every living thing in its path and carrying away much of the rigging. Staring into the mouth of one of the guns I could well imagine the terror of some unfortunate about to 'have a whiff of grapeshot'.

"All around the mound the ocean bottom lay strewn with the ping-pong-ball sized shot, rolling slowly back and forth in the constant surge of the ocean rollers as they broke above me. Also at a glance I could see hundreds of broken wine bottles, many still with the corks in place. I thought how the suffering castaways must have sat thirstily wondering about the fate of that part of the cargo! All around were large cannon balls, some a foot across – probably mortar shells – and some smaller cannon balls corroding away. Also beside the mound lay three long cylinders or 'cheeses' of rolled sheet lead." (Months later David was excited to find in London a manifest of valuables carried aboard the *Dodington* which included an entry that four "cheeses in lead" had been shipped to Mr William Walts of the English and Danish Missionaries, and that they were being carried "Freight free, being for the use of the above mentioned persons".

The lead was no doubt intended for church roofing.)

"I knew in those moments that I had found a big ship," said David. "Whether it was the *Dodington* or not would still have to be proved, but there was the wreck exactly as I had predicted, some considerable distance from the spot where legend had put her."

David shot to the surface to yell for Gerry to come and join him; but by this time Gerry had started a sweep behind the dinghy and was a hundred yards away. Excitedly David swam over to him and they both went back and dived to make a closer inspection of the find. They lifted several of the copper ingots in half an hour's survey during which they also carefully photographed the site and made notes of its bearings according to landmarks on shore. Then they gunned the outboard motor to hurry back to the landing stage and tell Gert Botha, who was aboard *Etosha*, of their discovery.

Determined to maintain absolute secrecy until the last possible moment, they invited Gert into the dinghy and took him half a mile out to sea to break the news so that none of *Etosha's* crew would overhear them. They also showed him the ingots. They then agreed to return to Port Elizabeth at once to get the sort of equipment they would need to lift the guns and copper and to sort out their legal position. That night they telephoned Mr John Wiley, a Cape Town Member of Parliament who had long been interested in maritime matters and with whom they had already discussed the implications of the *Sacramento* affair. Still fearing that their secret might leak out, they told Mr Wiley only that if he could come to Port Elizabeth they would have something of interest to tell him. He agreed that they should not talk about it on the phone and said he would fly to Port Elizabeth the next day. Two days later David and Mr Wiley went to the Port Elizabeth museum taking with them some of the ingots. There they spoke to the director, Dr John Wallace and the historian, Mrs Dee Nash, telling them what they had found. They said that they would salvage what they could of the cargo of the *Dodington*, and invited the museum to make a record of the affair. Before he flew back to Cape Town Mr Wiley also made an appointment for David and Gerry with a local lawyer, Mr Eric de Villiers, who proved to be extremely excited by the project and offered to act free of charge to protect their interests. Feeling they now had some measure of protection against other salvage divers and enthusiastic amateurs, they set about buying a considerable amount of equipment. This included a larger dinghy with two motors for use in poor conditions, and a compressor to be mounted aboard the *Etosha* so that their air bottles could be filled while they worked on the site. They also made up a number of aluminium salvage tags with their names stamped in the metal to show anyone else who came across the wreck that it was being actively worked. This gives no legal protection against poaching, but Eric believed it would be useful in establishing that they had found the wreck and were engaged in salvaging it should any other team try to do the same.

Chapter 10

On Saturday June 11 the party, together with Eric, sailed again for the island. As before, their equipment had been loaded aboard the *Etosha* with the utmost discretion. To inquirers they said they were conducting a survey of the jetty on the island and would probably be gone for some time. When they reached the island there was a westerly gale blowing, and only their sleeping bags and fresh meat could be safely taken ashore. The remainder of their supplies they left aboard *Etosha* to be moved when the weather moderated. David and Gerry went at once across the island to show Eric the wreck site, and were pleased to see that while the sea on that side was rough, it was not nearly as bad as they had feared. Little Dave meanwhile was sent to spear a fish for supper, a task from which he returned triumphant.

The next few days proved frustrating. The westerly gale continued unabated. But the party were able to fish, and they took Eric, who is a keen angler, to the outlying islands to give him some choice fishing. Some more essential supplies were taken off the *Etosha*, but in general the sombre weather, aggravated by rain, continued until the morning of June 15.

The day dawned with a light north-easterly wind whipping up only a moderate sea. The water round the island was clear as a bell. Gerry said, "When the conditions are good at the island they are incredible. The visibility under water can be anything up to twenty-five feet, which in this part of the Indian Ocean is fantastic. June 15 was such a day." Up with the sun, the men hurried through breakfast and changed into wet suits, taking Gert Botha out to *Etosha* before speeding toward the site in their dinghy. Meanwhile aboard the trawler an excited George Braxton pushed his engine throttles ahead and also steamed toward the site.

David and Gerry had already agreed that they would lift the cannon first, partly because these would provide the quickest and surest way of identifying the wreck, and also because they would be the easiest and quickest items to salvage. Once they had been salvaged *Etosha* could then be sent off about her proper business of commercial trawling.

From the dinghy Gerry and Little Dave plunged into the water with a buoy to make fast to the ship's anchor. This would then give them a working position almost in the centre of the site. As Gerry gasped in a lungful of air and prepared to go down with his snorkel, he spotted, for the first time, an eight foot Great White shark. His log book notes, "It was both an exciting and frightening experience to see this great animal so close and so unexpectedly". He immediately ordered Little Dave out of the water, feeling that with almost no experience of diving, let alone of diving among sharks, he would be safer in the dinghy. Gerry pressed on, made the buoy fast, and while swimming over the area spotted the unmistakable shape of a ship's bell seaward of the main mound of goods. Still using his snorkel, he dived and photographed it before swimming over to tell David. They decided to pull the bell to the surface quickly, and then get on with salvaging the cannon. It proved slightly more difficult than they had anticipated, but a good deal of heaving on a rope soon loosened the heavy bell, which broke surface shortly afterwards. Unfortunately it had broken into two long before it was salvaged and the middle piece, which would probably have borne the maker's, or even the ship's name, was missing. They were to spend many hours trying to recover that piece of circular metal, but in vain.

With the bell in the dinghy they prepared for the really hard work of lifting the guns, using a variation of a classic salvage technique which involves the use of camels. These are containers joined by a rope and fastened one on each side to the object to be lifted. Air is pumped into them, and provided the weight of the object and the amount of air pumped in have been correctly calculated, it will rise gently to the surface to be grappled or lifted from the water. With the concretions of 222 years surrounding the guns David and Gerry had no illusions that things would be that easy. They therefore took one of *Etosha's* trawl warps and made it fast to the gun they had decided to lift. They then put two fifty-pound plastic containers in position, stropped on the trawl warp, and filled the containers with compressed air. Nothing happened until they gave a signal on the light hand line between them and the trawler for *Etosha* to move slowly forward. As she did, the gun slowly broke loose and lifted just clear of the bottom of the camels. These however proved insufficient to lift the gun to the surface. While David kept an eye on the operation Gerry slowly began to guide the gun over the rocks and mounds in the sea bed to take it to deeper water where it could be hauled to the surface by the trawler's lifting gear.

The moment he began to do so a new danger presented itself. The surge of tide and waves around the shallow reefs threw Gerry from side to side, while the gun itself swung like a pendulum, sometimes moving so fast that he had to jump out of the way to avoid a body blow from the heavy bronze weapon. Once in deeper water, however, it was a mere bagatelle to get the gun on deck. To everyone's delight it turned out to be a perfectly preserved bronze howitzer, clearly bearing the initials of the King of England, George the Second, beneath a royal crown – exactly the right period for the *Dodington*.

Once the gun was on board Gerry and David leapt back into the water, intent on salvaging the bigger gun they had marked inshore of the howitzer. George Braxton and Gert Botha, both fired with enthusiasm, threw caution to the wind as they backed *Etosha* in over the reef to try to edge her directly above the gun for a straight lift – on this gun camels would be less than useless. Gerry and David then went down to strop the cannon. It took some doing because they had to move a number of copper plates which had fallen around it. Once stropped, a fresh problem arose when *Etosha's* winch proved incapable of budging the gun. As her stern sank under the strain, the anchor chain broke. Somewhat put out, Gerry started a long, slow manoeuvre which involved using a crowbar to shift the gun's position slightly. He thought this would make the lift easier, and it did; but a fresh problem arose as they guided the suspended gun into deeper water.

They had made the second strop fast over *Etosha's* bow, believing that this would provide a better purchase for the lift; but as the trawler moved out to sea the strop slipped, and the cannon dropped away into fifty feet of water. Both divers plunged down after it so as not to lose sight of the precious gun. Then the gun was laboriously winched to the surface without incident. It turned out to be a magnificent twelve-pounder, resplendent with the maker's name, Andrew Schalch, the date of founding, 1748, and a ducal as well as royal monogram, this last of George Rex.

While Gerry remained aboard *Etosha* to replenish their exhausted air supply, David, Little Dave, and an African crewman returned to the site in a dinghy to lift copper ingots. They had lifted twenty into the dinghy when David took a break in the day's work to swim close inshore and inspect the site further.

After finding another large anchor with a loose ring lying on the rocks he started back to *Etosha*. As he began to swim he realised that the odd swirl of the current, which sweeps away from the shore instead of towards it, had confused him. He was going the wrong way. To get back on the right track he backed towards a reef and started swimming towards a narrow gap between two large rocks. Once in the gap his eyes almost popped out with shock. A Great White shark fifteen feet long was swimming in at the far end. "It was an incredible moment," he said later. "My mind was racing through all sorts of alternatives including the possibility of photographing it – but I had the camera safety catch on. Then another shock: I found that with gloves on I could not work the safety catch of the shark banger. There was no alternative but to swim on and try to get past the shark hoping it would not attack me. In the event we passed one another with only feet to spare. These animals are totally unpredictable. It was a terrifying moment as I went past unable to see whether it intended turning and coming after me."

Happily the shark swam on and David returned hurriedly to *Etosha*, only to find that Gerry and Dave Smale had been "buzzed" by a Great White which they thought was probably the same shark. That lunchtime they christened the brute "Alfred" over a celebratory bottle of wine.

In the afternoon the sea became rougher. David decided that *Etosha* should stand off the island and that the compressor should be used to fill their airbottles while they took the big inflatable dinghy to the site. That afternoon they lifted half a ton of copper and found more bottles and musket balls. Then they began to use a particularly crafty device which they had designed specifically for the *Dodington* salvage. The three divers took cargo nets down to the ocean floor and pinned them down with copper ingots at the corners. Using crow bars they could then prize loose the rest of the copper and fill the nets ready for lifting aboard *Etosha*. The system had two advantages: in the first place they could load one and a half tons at a time; and in the second, when *Etosha* went off fishing or ferrying guano to Port Elizabeth the nets could be loaded and left on the sea bed for her to pick up on her return. In all it took two hours underwater to place the nets and fully load the first.

On the next diving day, June 17, they filled three nets and hauled one aboard *Etosha* before the wind came up and stopped operations. Though simple in theory the lifting operation did not go as smoothly as planned. The net was not brought aboard, but was left hanging over the bow as *Etosha* moved slowly out into open waters where the net could be more safely swung aboard. (Had this operation been carried out while rolling in the surf the trawler might have heeled right over because of the weight of the net.) In fact the net was not correctly stropped and banged dangerously against the trawler's bow, so that they had to lower it to the sea bed again and re-strop it before completing the operation.

During the loading of the nets they were again troubled by Alfred, who lurked not far from them all the while. "Alfred had a habit of creeping up on us" David recalls, "and we would then drop our crowbars and the ingots and swim towards him with the shark bangers, hoping to hell that the cartridge was dry and that he would turn tail in time." Despite his harassment Alfred was unable to stop them unearthing the treasures he had guarded so well. For that day they found a chest of penknives being shipped for trading purposes and the crystal remains of a splendid chandelier. As the pile of copper was shifted more and more of the *Dodington's* cargo came to light. David and Gerry became convinced, that as with the *Sacramento* the ship struck the outer edge of the reef in twelve feet of water, broke her back, and dropped most of her cargo through the bottom of the hold. The forward part of the ship was then driven farther across the reef and struck a second reef thirty yards closer inshore in seven feet of water, where the ship finally went to pieces. They concluded that the midships section, with its heavy cargo, stayed almost intact at the first strike, but that the bows and stern were ripped away by the giant breakers and driven to the position on Bird Island where the anchor finally landed.

This reconstruction of what happened from physical evidence on the ocean bottom is corroborated in precise detail by the *Public Advertiser* report of June 8, 1757 – which appeared almost exactly a year after the disaster to the day, and was unearthed in the British Museum in London after salvage work on the *Dodington* had been completed. Indeed, the site plan on which David and Gerry carefully noted the location of each item bore out Evan Jones's description of the ship sailing straight on to the reef and slewing over to starboard, for the heavier cannon and cargo remained splayed across the ocean floor on the outer reef while the rest was spread out ever farther inshore, driven there by those final fatal waves which put paid to the *Dodington*.

Two days later, on a halcyon morning with the sea as calm as it was ever to be off the island, they dived again, while *Etosha* sailed for harbour to fetch supplies. With much of the copper now shifted they began to find fabulously interesting artefacts. Says David, "Then we came across the stern, where there was a brass candlestick holder and a pair of compasses. In the midships section we discovered every imaginable type of trading goods. In some places pieces of stout old sea chests were still intact, but mostly the goods had fallen from the chests as they broke up and been formed over the centuries into clumsy conglomerates, welded together by sand and oxidation as well as coral. The conglomerates were in an eight inch deep layer on the ocean bottom, so that we had to break the layer loose to retrieve the goods and bring them, still in conglomerate form, to the surface to be carefully broken open. There were red, blue, green and white glazed beads; chests of knives including special ones for trimming pen quills, brass with bone inlays; clasp-knives with ornamental handles; long shaving blades and ordinary table knives with bone handles. In other chests we found brass-handled scissors; combs; delicately worked brass padlocks; clay smoking pipes; hand mirrors no doubt intended for use by the ladies of India. We even found still usable red lead paint and four sounding leads."

Also on the site they found pieces of muskets and pistols, ornamental brass trigger guards, flints, rifle and pistol balls. As each major item was brought up its relative position was carefully noted so that despite the awkward conditions the site could be as accurately marked and planned as possible.

As more and more of the cargo came to light the team began to be gripped by treasure fever. David explained what happened next. "Now, as things were getting more exciting, treasure fever caught us in its clasp. We knew that the survivors had saved a chest of the King's money and later rifled it. I had been brought up, like so many of us, to hear countless stories and read periodical newspaper reports on the *Dodington* treasure. Indeed, during the time spent in salvaging we had read two reports in different newspapers which referred to the *Dodington*. Little did their authors know that we were already salvaging her. I was positive that she would have more treasure on board.

"Then it happened! That Sunday when the *Etosha* had gone to port to fetch supplies, and with the waves crashing on to the wreck, one of the divers pulled himself on to the inflatable rubber dinghy and from his collecting bag poured a stream of silver pieces-of-eight into the bottom of the boat. Treasure! Picking up these coins we could immediately see that they were the Spanish pieces-of-eight so often described in the pirate tales of our youth, the coins Captain Kidd plundered, and Long John Silver's parrot immortalised. This was indeed treasure. The coins bore the names of either Philip or Ferdinand, and, in Spanish, 'King of Spain and India by the Grace of God'. From a quick examination we found all the coins to have been minted in the early 1700's, and none (thankfully,) later than the wrecking of the *Dodington*."

It turned out to be a good day for Gerry: no sooner had he discovered the ship's treasure than on an exploratory swim later in the day he found her galley – or at least the fire bricks of the furnace or stove and bric-à-brac which were all that remained of it. Near the bricks lay a copper pot lid and a number of musket balls as well as a great many beads.

But the day ended as far as diving went when Alfred, perhaps incensed that the treasure he had guarded so faithfully for so long had at last been snatched from him, became more aggressive than he had ever been before. He began swimming right up to the men, and on one occasion appeared only feet behind Gerry, who saw him only when he turned to see why a shadow had fallen across him. Gerry's log book reads, "Even though I swam down on him he wasn't at all alarmed, but moved off at a very leisurely pace".

During the next two days the weather prevented any diving on the site and the men waited, agonised, for it to moderate. Meanwhile they started the painstaking task of chipping the coins out of the concretions. It was a slow task, hard on the fingers and hard on the nerves. The slightest slip could damage either the coin or the worker's hand. At the same time Gerry decided to give Little Dave some experience of aqualung diving in less hazardous conditions, and together they swam out to the (incorrectly named) Dodington Rock. Gerry wrote in his log later, "Found the seaward side of the rock to be sheer and 80 feet or more deep. The pinnacles were very impressive and rather like fairytale mountains. We swam right round the rock but saw no wreckage. This dive confirmed our theory that the *Dodington* could never have struck here."

On June 21 the team dived again and filled the third cargo net with ingots ready for lifting. Then the weather really deteriorated and it became impossibly dangerous to dive on the *Dodington* site. For sixteen days they were obliged to while away the time diving off other parts of the island. They spent much time charting wrecks, finding in all ten ranging over several centuries.

A minor but irritating problem arose during this period when they discovered that one of the crew was drinking the methylated spirits used in the storm lanterns. The real difficulty was that once ashore he could hardly be trusted not to talk of the things he had seen brought up from the ocean. So far as they knew he had not seen the cannon or coin conglomerates, but they were determined to leave him ashore when they raised the copper ingots or anything else which might give the game away. In the event the man saw only a bronze fire-fighting water cannon from an old South African Railways tug, the *Fuller*, which went down near the island during the war. This was salvaged during a second period of bad weather, and provided the man with a story which he told around the harbour. From then on rumour mounted that David and Gerry had found the *Dodington*.

Far more alarming from a security point of view was something which was not confirmed until almost a year later: that while he was held in port by bad weather their skipper George Braxton was telling a local newspaper man precise details of the find. According to the reporter, Braxton virtually handed over his log book – a fact which would have led to his immediate dismissal had the team known of it. But the journalist found himself in an awkward position. He had only the one source of information; and even George had not been told categorically that the wreck was that of the *Dodington*, although it was a fair bet that it was. In the end, after lengthy discussion in the offices of *The Eastern Province Herald*, the story was shelved pending harder evidence. Braxton died of a heart attack before the salvage was completed.

As the southern hemisphere winter deepened the weather became steadily worse. The party on the island found themselves driven ashore for long stints, even running short of food when *Etosha* was several days overdue because of the appalling weather. On June 23 the westerly gales reached a peak of 40 knots, howling across the island, whipping up dust, driving indoors all but those who were duty bound to venture out. *Etosha* anchored off the island that day but dared not approach, and it was only the next day that supplies could be fetched over during a lull in the storm. The next day the gale freshened and rain beat down on the tiny community. Indoors Gerry worked on cleaning up the coins they had already freed of concretions, and set up some heavy duty batteries to clear them better by electrolysis. Meanwhile Little Dave busied himself stripping and cleaning the diving equipment. David spent hours poring over the survivors' accounts of the shipwreck looking for any further clues, and comparing their notes of the weather with the old lighthouse records. Strangely enough (although it was perhaps not strange for that mysterious island) no discernible pattern emerged; and as if to prove the point, next morning the wind died as quickly as it had risen so that the last of the supplies could be brought from the trawler and the men ashore had a welcome barbecue as a change from food cooked indoors. Meanwhile they were still unable to unload some scaffolding and building equipment for Oom Piet from *Etosha*, so the trawler continued to stand off the island in the hope of better conditions to come. On June 25 all three divers, David, Gerry and Little Dave, went out in the rubber dinghy to dive on various spots simply to break the tedium of remaining ashore.

Gerry recorded the day thus: "David and I did a deep dive (140 feet) seaward of the *Dodington* and found the bottom full of large potholes. All three of us then did another dive seaward of Dodington Rock. Two big shoals of yellowtail came past and we saw some really big Miss Lucy (a type of fish) and huge rock cod. We then had a look at North Patch but didn't see anything. Later found an iron ship. The sea bottom is covered in iron plating and only part of the stern looks like a ship's hull. David found some forks and bullet moulds. Decided that it must be the steamship *Western Hope* which sank at midnight on January 1, 1870."

Only on June 29 were the team able to unload the building material from *Etosha*. That night David decided to sail back to Port Elizabeth aboard her to consolidate various aspects of the salvage, not least of which would be to make arrangements with the customs officials to bring their salvage ashore in secret. On the island Gerry and Little Dave fretted, making occasional dives to keep their spirits up, and on one occasion standing transfixed as a water spout swirled past them. Gerry wrote, "It was very impressive as the sea seemed to be smoking and then the cloud dropped a long thin finger down that joined the spray from the water surface." So the days passed, until on July 5 *Etosha* returned with fresh supplies, and David with news of home and the world. They were still unable to dive on the site until July 8, though Gerry had religiously gone there every day hoping the weather might have altered. Also aboard *Etosha* was Dave Wratten, a friend of the team who apart from a lingering interest in the sea as a result of service in the Royal Navy was a handy and accurate sketcher. He set to work making notes and sketches of the island and the artefacts ashore.

The morning of July 8 the party rose to find the sea flat calm. They immediately decided to lift the nets full of copper ingots which were waiting on the bottom. To do this they asked George Braxton to put his boat in precisely the situation which had caused the loss of the *Dodington*.

The breakers roll in over the site from a mile and a half to seaward of the reef, recover themselves, and break a second time exactly over the site. To manoeuvre a single screw trawler in such conditions, and to hold it steady long enough to lift the nets, required not only skilled seamanship, but a high degree of courage. There was, of course, another complication. The divers would be underwater in the shallows stropping the nets, and once free of the bottom would swing as the waves took them. In other words they would have a copper pendulum weighing a ton and a half rising and falling above them as *Etosha* rode the swells – and at the same time swinging to and fro with the underwater movement of the breakers. It was not an enviable operation. There was, however, no alternative but to take a deep breath and get on with it. Though it was tricky, and at times came close to minor disaster, the operation went off smoothly enough. Soon all three of the ingot nets were safely aboard *Etosha* and a thankful George Braxton moved her quickly away from the "front" or sea side of the island and round to the shelter of the lee. (They also found a further two rolls of lead bringing the total to three, and under a pile of copper found but did not remove a third howitzer, dated 1755 like the rest.)

On July 10, after more bad weather, Gert Botha decided to use *Etosha's* echo sounder to try to find another well-known Bird Island wreck, the South African Railways harbour tug *Fuller* which sank during the Second World War. Having found what he thought to be the hulk, Gert dropped a buoy and Gerry and David slipped down sixty feet to find that the anchor of the buoy had dropped exactly on the wreck. Again Gerry's log notes: "The tug was on her starboard side and quite far from where she is supposed to have sunk. I tied a buoy to her cast iron propellers. It was quite spooky as the ship is whole. There were lots of port hole rings near the stern. The compass binnacle was missing from the bridge, but the engine room telegraph and wheel stanchions were still there. There were mess room plates and spoons as well as other eating utensils lying about." The tug must have sunk quickly because the crew seemed to have leapt up from a meal to abandon ship. The divers took some knives and forks for use in their island home, and what was even more unlikely, quantities of coal to keep their night fires going. They also brought up the water cannon which the drunken seaman mistook for a ship's gun of two centuries earlier.

On July 11 they returned to the *Dodington*, determined to raise the howitzer they had discovered beneath the copper. And at this point, before describing the actual operation, it may be explained that all the tools used, such as hammers and crowbars, were left underwater in stockpiles on the reef. In this way they saved themselves considerable energy in carrying heavy implements to and from the site after each working spell.

The raising of the howitzer proved a tricky business. The gun was concreted into the seabed by a combination of sandstone, rocks, coral and sea life. It was also surrounded by a deep pile of coal – as was a fairly large part of the site. No doubt the coal was to be used in the *Dodington's* galley; but there must have been enormous supplies on board, for to this day Oom Piet Odendaal and his men gather coal from the rocks along the island edge opposite the site for their own use.

In trying to raise the howitzer the divers had to winkle out of the way an iron gun which they took about ten yards out to sea. Then they dug under the howitzer with crowbars to strop it ready for lifting. When it was raised it proved to be in perfect condition like all the other guns salvaged from the site. The divers also lifted four more nets of copper before lunch while the crew were hard at it fishing over the side for their contribution to a splendid fish and chip meal. After lunch the team found another of the *Dodington's* sounding leads, and thought of the irony of the discovery – for had those heavy leads been used to sound the depth of water beneath her bottom the *Dodington* might never have struck. Even three miles off the island sounding would have shown them to be in a hundred feet of water; and this should have puzzled Mr Jones, who believed himself to be far out to sea. In the final mile and a half they would have been in approximately thirty feet of water, and this would certainly have sent the duty officer into a panic. Even then he might have had just enough time, despite the storm, to turn.

When they made a wider search of the site the team counted a total of twenty-six iron cannon splayed all over the area. These they purposely left behind. When iron guns such as those of the *Dodington* have been submerged for a couple of centuries they turn to dust shortly after being exposed to the air. Although one highly sophisticated unit at Portsmouth has developed a technique for preserving iron guns in these conditions the technique is not in common use; to lift the *Dodington's* iron guns would in David's opinion have been a form of sacrilege, for nothing meaningful could then be done with them. The team contented itself with noting their position on the site and making accurate descriptions of them.

On July 12 with the weather bad again the team decided to take a break. David and Gerry joined the crew of *Etosha* as she headed for port heavily laden with salvage they had decided to shift to the mainland. Aboard *Etosha* were the cannons, the three lead rolls, and twelve tons of copper. All had to be declared through customs and correctly checked before it could be locked away in an approved storage space which would also be checked by customs officials. By radio the team notified Eric de Villiers of their intention and he contacted customs as had previously been arranged. After some consideration it was decided to leave the salvage locked in *Etosha's* hold for three nights to allay the suspicions of the Press and others on the harbour who were only too keen to know why David and Gerry had returned. Then, at 10 pm at night, *Etosha* was stealthily moved to a cargo berth in the harbour where a crane could be used to lift the heavy goods from her hold. With five men working in the hold and another five on the eight-ton truck which had been ordered for the purpose, the operation was swiftly completed. At the customs check point the team was astonished to find that the weigh-bridge showed they had brought fourteen tons of salvage ashore. From there they drove to the outskirts of Port Elizabeth, where the customs officials had agreed that the salvage could be stored in Gert's lock-up garage provided it was sufficiently secure. With an official noting every item as it came off the truck the men manually unloaded everything; only as dawn tinged the sky did they get into David's car to drive home to bed. However they were well satisfied that apart from a few railway workers who had shown little interest, no one knew that they had successfully landed the first of *Dodington's* treasure.

Throughout the latter part of July the weather remained constantly foul and the team, having returned to the island, found themselves sinking into the sort of black depression which must have overcome the *Dodington* crew. Worse, they also found themselves angry with one another and losing their tempers over minor irritations. This was only to be expected with enforced idleness and having to live at such close quarters for so long; but luckily each member of the party knew he must contain his pent-up feelings – it would be dangerous to dive on such a tricky project if there was ill-feeling in the team.

Etosha had arrived back at the island with a four-ton cement block on deck intended for use as a mooring, but it took several days to unload it because of continuing storms. On July 17, the 222nd anniversary of the *Dodington* wreck, David and his team sat on the rocks opposite the site and watched the sea rush forward, picturing to themselves how the ship must have been pitched headlong on to those craggy reefs, her bows finally ending almost on shore. On July 27 it was a dispirited team which celebrated Little Dave's birthday; to compound the aggravation of inactivity David had a stomach upset and Gert was beginning to complain that he had been at the island too long and wanted to go back to harbour to carry out some minor repairs on *Etosha*.

Their next dive on the *Dodington* was on July 28. Gerry noted: "Wind easterly and the swell down a little, but still rough. David didn't feel up to diving and Gert offered to take his place. Rather a desperate effort on his part to get something done. We decided it was unwise to risk our reputations by losing a diver (he was very inexperienced) so we put him off."

In the event Gerry and Little Dave were able to load two nets with ingots that day and Gerry found two bone-handled knives intended for trading in India, a trigger guard from a pistol, innumerable musket balls, some flints, and a long copper cylinder. Later the weather again deteriorated and Gert sailed *Etosha* at 11 pm heading back to Port Elizabeth.

Once more the team was obliged to wait impatiently for the weather to clear up. This time they were forced to spend much of the time indoors reading books; the gales were so bad there was little point in going outside. Occasionally they dived in deeper water for the sake of relief from the monotony, but by August 9, when *Etosha* again returned with fresh supplies, they decided to sail back to Port Elizabeth in her. Both David and Gerry felt there were more worth-while chores to be done there than on the gale-swept island.

They returned to the island in mid-August and helped the island men load guano on to the *Etosha*. They also dug on what they believed to be the survivors' land site, where they unearthed bits of lead, nails, and what appeared to be iron shot.

The last dive on the *Dodington* for that expedition came on August 20, when the wind fell to a light westerly breeze. With David concentrating on taking underwater photographs, Gerry and Litte Dave hastily loaded another net of copper ingots. In between working on the net Gerry swam into the shallows, locating several cannon as he went. These were iron guns which for reasons already given could not be brought to the surface. In all Gerry noted that they had located twenty-three cannon on the site, and by the time they left there were a total of twenty-six on their site plan.

After locating three small anchors and some more pieces-of-eight, the team returned to the dinghy, only to be swamped by two large waves. Annoyed, they returned to base to refill their aqualungs; and then hastened back to the site, where all three filled yet another net with ingots. That night *Etosha* sailed for Port Elizabeth, carrying the day's finds with her, and taking Little Dave for a well-earned shore leave.

With nothing to do but fish and make odd dives around the island David and Gerry settled into the dull routine which tends to dominate the place. The only spark of excitement was a visit from the lighthouse maintenance staff and a scheduled visit from a party of people who were studying the penguins. They were disconcerted to learn from the second party that they had been told by the museum what the team was really doing on the island. This worried them. As the project was supposed to be top secret David and Gerry were extremely angry, and prayed that not too much damage had been done by people talking in Port Elizabeth. As it was, a young reporter from one of the local newspapers had quizzed them about their activities on the lighthouse radio-phone, but they succeeded in referring him to Eric and cutting the conversation short. However it seemed that the operation had been truly "blown" when another reporter phoned the next day, September 1, to ask for their comment on his story (as yet unprinted) that they had been unloading cannon and copper in Port Elizabeth. Once more they referred the call to Eric, who phoned later to suggest that David should fly back on the first helicopter flight next day. The helicopter was once more ferrying lighthouse men to and from the island, and would be busy shuttling between there and the airport all day. David agreed, and left early next morning for an urgent meeting with Eric.

In the event the Press held off because of consistent "no comments" from the whole team, though as it transpired one local paper at least had substantial evidence for a story which included some of the original survivors' accounts.

By mid-September Gert decided that he would take no further part in the *Dodington* operation. After some discussion it was agreed to raise the remaining nets and abandon the site as far as he was concerned. So on September 17, in dangerous conditions, and a heavy swell, the old *Etosha* backed on to the site for the last time to lift the remaining three nets of ingots to her deck. That night David, Gerry and Little Dave invited Kallie the cook and Jack for a roast

Chapter 11

Though the excitement of the chase had long since died there remained for David the thrill of the detective work to remove any shadow of doubt that he had found the *Dodington*. That he had found the first British East Indiaman ever salvaged there was no question of doubt – the evidence of the trading goods and the monograms on the guns left no room for argument. In favour of her being the *Dodington* was the fact that she was the only British East Indiaman known for certain to have been wrecked on Bird Island. But more important than this was the technique by which she was found. No archaeologist would doubt that the strongest possible case had already been made on the day the ship was found, because David had already been able to predict her position to within a few yards from his library studies and knowledge of the area. For him to have done this, and then to have found her within minutes, was proof enough that this was the *Dodington*: it would have been a one in a million chance for another British Indiaman to have struck just that very spot.

Final identification would come through the guns, which because of their mid-eighteenth-century date would be fairly easily identified, not only in themselves, but also as to the ship in which they were carried. This was particularly so in the case of the East India Company, which severely limited the weapons carried as cargo aboard its armed merchantmen for fear that both vessel and cargo might fall into the hands of the enemy.

Having cleaned up the four *Dodington* guns, David's team found that the three howitzers bore the name of the founder, Richard Gilpin, the date of casting 1755, the crown and monogram of King George II, and the initial L encircled by the motto of the Knight Commanders of the Order of the Bath, *Tria juncta in uno* a fact which particularly amused David as it was also the motto of his school, Grey High School, Port Elizabeth. The inscription on the twelve pounder showed that it was cast in 1748 by Andrew Schalch. It bore the King's monogram and crown, but higher up the barrel under a ducal crown the monogram M. All this information, together with· sketches and measurements, was sent by David to Mrs Dee Nash at the Port Elizabeth museum. She in turn wrote to the Greenwich Maritime Museum and Mr H. L. Blackmore, Keeper of Firearms in the Armouries of the Tower of London. She also wrote to the East India Office in London, hoping for a bill of lading or cargo manifest of the *Dodington*.

In reply Mr Blackmore had this to say about the howitzers. "The L is for John 1st Viscount Ligonier who was Lieut. General of the Ordnance 1748-57 and Master General 1759-63. The motto is that of the Order of the Bath of whom Ligonier was a Knight. We know very little of Richard Gilpin except that he had a foundry in the Borough of Southwark, London, and was a contractor to the Board of Ordnance in the middle of the 18th century. He is reported to have died in 1772."

David's brother Geoffrey, when working as a journalist in London, later found out that the monogram M was that of John, second Duke of Montagu, who inherited the title in 1705, became Master General of the Ordnance in 1740, relinquished the post in February 1742 for some inexplicable reason only to take it up again in the next month, and to continue in office until his death on July 6, 1749.

More is known about Schalch than Richard Gilpin. According to the *Dictionary of National Biography,* which describes him as a master-founder, he was born in 1692 at Schaffhausen. After being employed in the cannon foundry at Douay he came to England, and in August 1716 was engaged to build the furnaces and provide the utensils for the new brass foundry at Woolwich.

Up to that time the only place for casting brass ordnance in England was Bayley's private foundry in Moorfields. The *Dictionary* records that a number of people assembled there on 10 May 1716 to see some of the French guns taken by Marlborough recast as English pieces, and an explosion occurred by which seventeen persons were killed and others injured. It was in consequence of this disastrous accident that a government foundry was decided on. The story has often been repeated that Schalch, a young and unknown man, predicted this explosion, having noticed the dampness of the moulds; that after it had taken place he was advertised for, and that the selection of a site for the new foundry was left to him. He has therefore been reckoned the father of the Woolwich Arsenal.

The story is however unauthenticated. No such advertisement has been traced. On the contrary, one has been found (10 July 1716) inviting competent men to offer themselves, after the site had been chosen and the building begun. A good report of Schalch's capacity having been obtained through the British minister at Brussels, his appointment to Woolwich was confirmed in October.

Schalch remained master-founder for nearly sixty years, acquiring wealth and reputation; and never suffered the furnaces to be opened till workmen and spectators had joined him in prayer. He died in 1776 at the age of eighty-four, and was buried in Woolwich churchyard. Four of his grandsons in the Royal Artillery were commemorated with him in 1864 by a window in St. George's (garrison) Church at Woolwich.

This information brought to our notice by the Maritime Museum, helped to build up a history of the cannon; but it was not until Mrs Nash received another letter, this time from the East India Office, that the Port Elizabeth Museum authorities would allow that David had, as he had told them six month before, found the *Dodington*.

It is not clear precisely how much information Mrs Nash obtained on the *Dodington*. Thus in the case of the letter from Mr Blackmore she typed extracts, but omitted some of the information provided, as Mr Blackmore was later to confirm. She was however told by the East India Office that the *Dodington* carried twenty-six guns in her own battery and that between them the *Eastcourt, Duke of Dorset* and *Dodington* were to carry two twelve-pounders, ten six-pounders and four five-and-a-half inch howitzers for Fort St George. David found the information interesting but hardly conclusive because any one of the ships could have carried any combination of the pieces. Finding difficulty in obtaining information in Port Elizabeth he decided that the fastest and most thorough way of obtaining it was to go to the fountain-head, which in the case of both ships meant an expensive flight to London with its treasure chest of libraries, records and international academic authorities. Accordingly he flew to Britain on New Year's day 1978 to spend five weeks in an exhaustive round of research and meetings.

Almost at once he was introduced to Mr Tony Farrington, Director of the East India Office, and Dr K. N. Chaudhuri of the Department of History at the London School of Oriental and African Studies, the world expert on British East Indiamen. Together they proved David to be correct in his identification of the *Dodington* by providing him with the manifest of the ship and the Company orders and instructions to Fort St George, which last contained this crucial passage: "His Majesty having been graciously pleased to give directions to the Board of Ordnance to furnish the Company with the following Brass Ordnance Viz^t. Two twelve pounders and ten six pounders cannon and four howitzers of five inches and an half ... We now send and consign to you on the ships Eastcourt and Duke of Doresett ten of the said six pounders ... the remainder we intend to send you by the Dodington ..."

Little further proof was now needed, yet there was plenty more to come. The ship's manifest recorded that the *Dodington* carried forty iron guns, of which he had counted twenty-six on the seabed at the island; forty-one cases of copper each containing 1,352 plates; and 2,207 "single heads of barbary copper moulded into a circular shape". But David could hardly contain himself when he read later in the list that the *Dodington* was also carrying two "rubbing stones" or what we would now call grindstones; and both of these he knew to be safely in his home together with the cheeses of lead he had found. From that moment it was no longer a matter of

Appendix I

A MANIFEST OF GOODS MERCHANDIZE AND FOREIGN SILVER LICENCED BY THE COMMITTEE OF SHIPPING OF THE COURT OF DIRECTORS OF THE UNITED EAST INDIA COMPANY LADEN ON BOARD THE SHIP DODINGTON CAPTAIN JAMES SAMSON COMMANDER BOUND FOR FORT ST, GEORGE BY THE SEVERAL PERSONS AS FOLLOWS VIZt.

CAPTAIN JAMES SAMSON.

J S						£100	–	–
	1	at	5	Two Case Looking Glasses		£100	–	–
	1		2	Two Chests Amber Beads and a small box in one of the Said Chests qt. some Coral		400	–	–
	20	at	41	Twenty-two Barrells Glass Beads		400	–	–
	4	at	19	Sixteen Casks qt Madder Root		150	–	–
	1	at	5	Two Cases Glass Ware		100	–	–
				One Case qt. two Table Clocks				
				Two do. Clock Work and Dolls for the Movements		80	–	–
			3	One Runlet of Vermillion		50	–	–
	1		2	Two Chests Cutlery		200	–	–
	1	at	4	Three Cases pickles and One Chest of sweet Oil		40	–	–
				One Case qt. Telliscopes		32	–	–
				One do. six Remnants Cloth each six Yards		30	–	–
				Two Boxes Gold thread		300	–	–
				One Cable of 8 In. Six Ransers from 4 to 5 Inc. Three Coils 3½, Hons Coild. In., in all 82 Tons ½		85	–	–
				Eighty Whole Haggots of Steel 4 tons		120	–	–
	1	at	18	Eighteen Casks qt. 6 tons Red head		140	–	–
				Twenty anchors from 1ce to 2ce				
				Twenty hour Grapnells of ½ to 2ce in all 3 tons		100	–	–
				On his indulgence				
	1		2	Two Firkins qt. Flints				
	3		6	Four Cases small arms				
	7	at	14	Eight Baggs each qt ½				

Which are to be sold Madagascar, or delivered to the Govt. and Council at Fort St. George at prime Cost.

E J				Mr. EVAN JONES CHIEF MATE				
				One box Gold thread		100	–	–
	1			One Chest Cutlery		40	–	–
	1	at	3	Three Cases Looking Glasses		30	–	–
	1	at	4	Four Bales qt. 18 Bolts of Canvas		128	–	–
				On his Indulgence				

Mr. MELES TOBETWOOD, MIDSHIPMAN

C.F.M.F.	Two Boxes of Cutlery	£40	–	–

Mr. JOHN RAY, PURSER

J R	1	at	7	Seven Cases of Looking Glasses	140	–	–

Mr. Charles Cunningham, Surgeon

C C	One Chest Cutlery	25 — —
	One Case Hatts	25 — —
	One do. Looking Glasses	10 — —
	One do. Prints	7 — —
	One do. Stationary	5 — —

Mr. William Webb, 3d. Mate

W W	One Hhhd Glass Ware	20 — —
	One Chest Cutlery	58 — —
	One Box Snuff	5 — —
	One Half Chest Wine	9 — —

Mr. John Collett, 2d. Mate

J C	Two Cases of Glass Lanthorns	20 — —
	Two do. Glass Ware	30 — —
	One do. Cutlery	60 — —
	One do. Saffron	50 — —
	One do. Tobacco	6 — —
	Iron ware 10ce in two Casks	20 — —

On their Indulgences.

Mr. John Le Gross to Capt. John Brchier.
Directed
One Box Books

Mr. James Spaggs to Mr. Thomas Coales.

do. One Box of sundry Necessaries for Wearing Apparrell.

Mr. Wm. Walts to the English and Danish Missionaries

D M
        1 at 3 Three Chests qt. Stationary, 25th Glue, some pot
E M   Ash, Indigo, and Sundrys.

        4   5 Two Cheeses in Lead
               6 One Chest of Books
               7 One Chest Stationary, Sage and Sundrys.
        8   9 Two Cheeses in Lead
                  Freight free being for the Use of the abovementioned
                     Persons.

General Sinclair to Mr. Alexander Darylmple.

Directed One Box of Books
One do. Sweatmeats.
One do. Apparrell and necessarys
Freight free being for his own Use.

Mr. Abraham Dafonseca

A F	1	One Box Coral & Beads	800 — —
C		Consigned to Messrs. Ins. Walsh and Henry Vansittart	
		On which he has paid Freight and Permission and given Bond pursuant to Order of Court.	

East India House,
London, the 28th March 1755.

Appendix II

No. 31

Manifest of private gold silver and wrought plate Lycenced to be shipped on Board the Doddington for Fort St. George on account of the following persons vizt.

	OZr.	DW.
For Robert Clive Esqr. Governor for Fort St. David		
One Chest of Gold, Marked R.C. No. 1 qt.	653	6 –
The Missionaries on the Coast in Silver–		
One Chest D.M.Z. No. 8	1,870	– –
Do. E.M.F. No. 15	1,311	– –
Do. E.M.K. No. 16	1,385	– –
Messrs. Walsh and Vansittart Do. G No. 1	3,258	5 –
John Barrons Commissary and Paymaster to the Train of Artillery		
Do. J.B. No. 1...	3,663	– –
Capt. Francis Ford to the Commanding Officer in being of Colonel		
Adlercrons		
Regiment Five Chests Marked J.A.No. 1 at 5	18,591	– –
Chas. Boddam Esqr. a Case of Wrought Plate ...C.B.	444	– –
	OZ 31,175	11 –

BULLION OFFICE   THOS. WEBB
EAST INDIA HOUSE
29th MARCH 1755

Appendix III

1754

A LIST OF MILITARY OFFICERS AND SOLDIERS ON BOARD THE SHIP
DODINGTON CAPTAIN JAMES SAMSON COMMANDER FOR FORT ST. GEORGE
No 38

Names.	Quality.	Country	Trade.	Age
CHARLES PRISSICK	Lieutenant	Yorkshire	Gentleman	30
ALEXR. CAMERON	Do.	Scotland	Do	28
ANEAS SUTHERLAND	Do.	Scotland	Do.	28
[SIC]	Cadet	Durham	Do.	22
ANDREW NESBILL	Do.	Ireland	Do.	22
ROBERT CAMPBELL	Do.	Scotland	Do.	21
THOMAS SHELDON	Soldier	Chesire	Labourer	22
WILLIAM HUMPHREY	Do.	Salop	Do.	20
ROBERT BARNES DISOBd	Do.	Birmingham	Button-maker	17
THEOPLULUS STEVENS	Do.	Salop	Labourer	19
THOMAS PEAST DISCHd	Do.	Cheshire	Smith	27
JOHN HODGSON	Do.	Staffordshire	White Smith	23
SAMUEL PEARSE	Do.	Chesire	Smith	23
LOVEDAY SMOKE	Do.	Oxon	Weaver	24
JOHN DALE	Do.	Yorkshire	Marine	30
RALPH MORT	Do.	London	Bricklayer	27
DAN MC. KINNAN	Do.	Scotland	Soldier	23
JOHN PEARCE	Do.	Gloucestershire	Labourer	18
ROGER BOYDEN	Do.	Suffolk	Baker	18
ISAAC PAYNE	Do.	Do.	Do	16
JOHN WALKINS	Do.	[Sic]	Taylor	31
ADAM CAREEFF	Do.	Susses	Shoe-maker	23
TIMOTHY BOULAN DISCHd	Do	Ireland	Taylor	26
CHARLES DUNSTON	Do.	Leicestershire	Wool Comber	18
MATHIAS PEARTREE	Do.	London	Weaver	24
JAMES CRATON	Do.	Dublin	Plush Weaver	28
JOHN DOWELL RUN	Do.	Do.	Carpenter	25
JOSEPH WARDE	Do.	Yorkshire	Cutler	22
JOHN PARKHAM	Do.	London	Joiner	32
ROBt DAVION	Do.	Bucks	Cabinet-maker	22
ROBt. WILKINSON	Soldier	Westmoreland	Labour	31
WILLIAM HICCOCK	Do.	[. . .]	Do.	17
RICHARD WALKER	Do.	[. . .]	Do.	17
GEORGE HEATH	Do.	[. . .]	Do.	17
ROWLAND MORGAN	Do.	[. . .]	Rope-maker	21
THOMAS LISBY	Do.	[. . .]	Labourer	21
THOMAS ADAMS	Do.	[. . .]	Do.	17
WILLIAM EVANS	Do.	[. . .]		18
JAMES SOLEWEATHER DISCHd	Do.	Suffolk	Labourer	19
JOHN MILLS	Do.	Gloucestershire	Do	25
WILLIAM BOULTON	Do.	Wilts	Do.	19
WILLIAM NEALE DISCHd.	Do.	Somersetshire.	Weaver	22
JOHN ORAM	Do.	London	Labourer	18
THOs. MARTIN	Do.	Staffordshire.	Do.	22
JOHN WARD DISCHd.	Do.	Norfolk	Shoe-Maker	25
THOs. HOE	Do.	London	Weaver	30
JOSEPH LATON	Do.	Birmingham	CurryCombMaker	18
THOMAS DAVIS	Do.	Wales	Labourer	18
WILLIAM MORTIENORE	Do.	Oxon	Do.	24
JOSEPH WITTON	Do.	London	Do.	26

THOS. PUGH RUN	Do.	Ireland	Flax Dresser	20
ABRAHAM GROUT	Dop.	London	Peruke Maker	30
JOHN HASLIP	Do.	Essex	Labour	28
JOHN MAIDS	Do.	Nottinghamshire	Do.	21
JOHN ETHERINGTON	Do.	Salop	Do.	18
DUNCAN CAMPBELL	Do	Edinburgh	Do.	18
BENJAMIN LEVIS	Do.	Nottingham	Weaver	22
JOHN BROUGHTON DISCHd.	Do.	Bucks	Baker	19
RICHARD HOLT	Do.	Kerts	Labourer	16
THOS. WINWRIGHT	Do.	London	Do.	17
JOSEPH WORTHEY	Do.	Hertford	Do.	24
FRANCIS PROUT	Do.	Gloucestershire	Do.	18
THOMAS EMMERSON	Do.	London	Gardner	21
JAMES RATFORD DISCHd.	Do.	York	Taylor	25
THOMAS COLLEY	Do.	Lincolnshire	Cork Cutter	20
THOMAS FOSTER	Do.	[. . . .]	Wool Beater	30
WILLIAM KATE	Do.	Kent	Labourer	18
WILLIAM ALLEN DISCHd.	Do.	Goucester	Do.	26
AUGUSTINE MADEVILL	Do.	Lincolnshire	Barber	29
JOHN KEMP	Do.	Deronshire	Labour	26
WILLIAM MELLINS	Do.	Oxon	Weaver	19
RICHARD PURDUE	Do.	Plymouth	Do.	25
WILLIAM HUNT	Do.	London	Turner	26
JOHN WINDLEY	Do.	Derby	Wool Comber	19
NATHANIEL EVANS	Do.	London	Gardner	16
JOHN CASTON	Do.	Ireland	Labourer	21
WILLIAM FOWLER	Do.	Salop	Shoe-maker	25
JOHN DAWNEY	Do.	London	Glover	17
WILLIAM POPE	Do.	Do.	Weaver	27
JOHN COOK	Do.	Stufford	Labourer	17
WILLIAM RAWLEY	Do.	Do.	Smith	27
WILLIAM BISHOP	Do.	[. . . .]	[Sic]thecary	27
THOMAS RALTON	Soldier	[. . . .]	Weaver	17
JOHN KELLET	Do.	Surry	Glass Grinder	20
JAMES JAMES	Do.	Somersetshire	Shoe-maker	18
WILLIAM JONES	Do	Wales	Labourer	18
JOSEPH DIXON	Do.	Ireland	Do.	30
JONATHAN LIGHT	Do.	Surry	Do.	18
ANDREW BULL	Do.	Huntingtonshire	Do.	23
WILLIAM GOSTELOW	Do.	London	Do.	17
CHARLES BISCUM	Do.	Westminster	Do.	17
JOHN FLETCHER	Do.	Surry	Turner	26
RICHARD SANSBURY DISCHd.	Do.	London	Labourer	21
THOMAS DUNCAN DISCHd.	Do.	Scotland	Do.	17
WILLIAM GLAN DISCHd	Do.	Do.	Do.	18

EAST INDIA HOUSE,
  LONDON THE 28th MARCH 1755.

G. HIGGINSON.

N.B.–James Measures a Deserter from the Third Regiment of Guards takes Passage "by his Majesty's Command" on this Ship, to be incorporated in Colonel John Adlercron's Regiment.

G. HIGGINSON.

Appendix IV

No. 7.

LIST OF THE COMPANYS PACKET TO FORT St. GEORGE
BY THE SHIP DODINGTON.

1. The Companys General Letter to Fort St. George dated the 26th March 1755.
2. Copy Companys Additional General Letter to Fort St. George dated the 14th February 1755.
3. Triplicate of the Companys General Letter to Fort St. George sent [[per]] Eastcourt and Duke of Dorset dated the 31st January 1755.
4. Packet from the Secret Committee directed to the Hon'ble the President and Council for all the Forces and Affairs of the English Nation at Fort St. George.
5. Packet from the Secret Committee directed to the Hon'ble the Governor for the time being of Fort St. George [[per]] Dodington. To be received from Captain Samson it being enclosed with the Companys Packet to him.
6. Invoice of the Dodington for Fort St. George Amounting to £1756-13.
7. Bill of Loading of Do.
8. Invoice of the Dodington for Bengal Amounting to £3590-0-10.
9. Bill of Loading of Do.
10. Invoice of the Ordnance and Stores shipped on board the Dodington for Fort St. George.
11. Bill of Loading of Do.
12. Account of the value of the Ordnance and Artillery stores shipped on Board the Eastcourt Duke of Dorset and Dodington Amounting to £1783-13-6.
13. The Companys Indulgence.
14. Charterparty of the Ship Dodington.
15. Copy of the Companys Instructions to Captain James Samson.
16. Copy of the Companys additional Orders to him. The Three last to be forwarded with the Ship.
17. Account of Coral Licensed to be shipped on board the Dodington for Fort St. George to purchase Diamonds.
18. List of Persons licensed to proceed to and remain in the Advices [[per]]Eastcourt and Duke of Dorset particularizing those who are under security not to be chargeable there. Both signed by the Secretary.
19. Manifest of Private silver licensed to be shipped the Dodington for Fort St. George.
20. Manifest of Goods and Merchandize licensed to be shipped on board the Dodington for Fort St. George.
21. Copy of the Dodington's Victualling Bill.
22. List of 3 Officers and 77 soldiers on board the Dodington with an account of their Country Age and Occupation
23* Establishment and Pay of a Company of Artillery in His Majesty's Service.
24* Account of the Tower Weight and Assays of Coins received from Fort St. George [[per]] Dragon.
25* Covenants of Mr. Edmund Maskelyne Junior Merchant at Fort St. George to be dated executed, witnessed and returned by the first Ship after the Board shall have called upon him to re-enter the Civil Service.
26* Patterns of 1 Bale of White Flannels No. 2 W.F. [[per]] Dodington for Fort St. George.
27. Packet directed to the Hon'ble the President and Council for all the Forces and Affairs of the English Nation at Fort William in Bengal [[per]] Dodington.
    *Nos. 23, 24, 25, 26, were lost.

Appendix V

ORDERS AND INSTRUCTIONS GIVEN BY THE COURT OF DIRECTORS OF THE UNITED COMPANY OF MERCHANTS OF ENGLAND TRADING TO THE EAST INDIES TO CAPTAIN JAMES SAMSON COMMANDER OF THE SHIP DODINGTON, OR TO THE COMMANDER FOR THE TIME BEING.

1. We the said Court of Directors having hired and Freighted the Ship Dodington whereof you are Commander to serve us for the fun from England to Fort St. George on the Coast of Choromandel, Fort William in Bengal, and to such other Ports or Places in the East Indies whereunto you shall be directed to therefore hereby order you, as soon as [. . . . . .] to make all possible Expedition that winds and weather shall permit directly for Fort St. George aforesaid whereto you are first consigned.

2. On your arrival at Fort St. George you are to deliver to our President and Council there all the Packets directed to them, with all the Bullion, Goods and Merchandizes on Board consigned thither, you are to land all the Passengers and Soldiers, and in all things according to your Charter-Party (a [. . . . .] whereof is delivered to you for your strict observation whereof) to follow from time to time the Orders of our said President and Council for your further proceeding [. . . .] President and Counncil of Fort St. George [. . . . .] Fort William in Bengal, you [. . . . .]those orders, and on your [. . . . .]and [. . . . . . .]Council there, all such Packets, Bullion, from Fort St. George, and you are then to follow the Orders of Our said President and Council of Fort William for your further Proceedings.

3. We strictly require you to keep up the Worship of God on Board your Ship and good Orders among your Men, taking care of their health during the whole Voyage, take care of all Passengers and Soldiers that We have sent or shall send on board, be very tender of Our Soldiers health give them daily fitting Provisions, keep them stirring and in Motion to prevent the Scurvy, and other Distempers, but We will not have them made the Drudges of the Ship.

4. You must carry with you Mediteranean Pass there being many Algerine Rivers [[?reivers, or robbers]] abroad, which you may meet with in your Passage you must carry with you the full [. . . . . . .]of English Mariners according to the direction of the Act of Navigation and your Covenant in Charterparty.

5. Whatever Stationary is or shall be sent on board your Ship by Us, must be put into the Breadroom or other dry Place in the Hold abast [[?abaft]] the Main Mast but not in any moist Place, lest it be thereby spoiled as Our Advices from India have often complained. Keep all our Packets in the Round House free from Damp.

6. We possitively require and Order that you do not directly or indirectly either for yourself or any other Person, carry out any Bullion Goods or Merchandizes, or any Letters but what you shall be *agreed* by us or some Committee appointed by Us [. . . . .] shall license you to carry and that you [. . . . . .] to prevent all your Officers and carry out Bullion, Goods, Merchandizes [. . . .] without the like License.

7. Put your Ship in the best Posture of Defence Quarter your Men, and frequently excercise them at the Great Guns and with Small Arms to make them expert upon all necessary Occasion inserting in the Logg Book the times when they are excercised. Trust no Colours, and avoid Speaking to any Ship at Sea, and in general be constantly on your Guard.

8. You are in the whole Course of your Voyage to have a Clear Ship and be in all respects ready for an immediate Engagement in case you should be attacked by Pirates, and you are to keep your Ship in the best Posture of Defence until you get safe to your last consigned Port.

9 Make no deviation or touch at any Place but where you are [. . . . . .] or allowed unless it shall be absolutely necessary for the recovery of your Sick People or the preservation of you Ship and Cargo and even then not without the Advice and Consent in Writing of the Majority in a regular Consultation of Yourself and Officers to be duly held on the Occasion.

10. Take every Opportunity until your arrival at your last Consigned Port of advising us of all your Proceedings and of every Occurrence worthy and notice, directing your letters to the Secretary, those by Dutch Ships must be under Cover to Messers. George Clifford and Sons Merchants at Amsterdam.

11. Exact Journals of all Transactions and Occurrances during the whole Voyage are to be kept by yourself and Officers which are to be delivered to Our Governor and Council of the Settlement whenever the Durington shall be discharged our Service, The Logg Book delivered you from hence must be strictly kept according to the directions prefixed therein and is to be given in it [. . . .] with the Journals.

102

12. [..........] particular [..........] in your Journal of all [...................] and whatever may occur to [.......... ....] known, and which may lend to the general knowledge and Improvement of the Navigation to and in the East Indies, you are to point out the same in writing to Our Governor and Council of the Settlement whereat the Ships last Consignment shall be unladed, to be transmitted to us that it may be Registered in a Book We have directed to be kept for that purpose.

13. In case you are furnished with any Stores out of His Majesty's Yards or Ships of War send us by the two first Conveyances an Exact Account of what you receive when and where they were delivered to you and by whom.

14. We possitively forbid your Suffering the Men to run out more than One third of their Wages upon any pretence whatsoever.

15. You are upon no Account whatsoever to take or admit on board your Ship to be carried to or towards the East Indies any Person or Persons who shall not have the Company [................] of the proper Office.

16. The Boatsman or in his Absence the Superior Officer on board is to enter in a Book for that purpose delivered to you a True and Perfect Account of every Parcel Goods received into or delivered out of the Ship as well belonging to the Company as others together with the Marks and Numbers thereof to be delivered to the Governor and Council of the Ships last Consigned Ports.

17. You or Your Purser must Sign Bills of Lading for all Treasure, Goods and Merchandize Shipped on board for Our Account.

18. We have put on board the Gallons of Brandy for each Soldier, which must be duly distributed among them in proper quantities for their refreshment and support.

19. You are hereby Liberty Ordered to receive no Commissions from or be any Wages aiding or Assisting to Foreigners in carrying on any Trade for them within the Limits of Our Charter, as you will Subject yourself to Our Greatest displeasure if you shall be guilty of a breach of this Order.

20. Our Secret Committee for this Year are Roger Drake, Richard Chauney, William Mabbott and Jones Raymond Esquires, You are hereby directed to follow all such Orders as you shall receive from those Gentlemen or any Three of them relating to Signals and Places of Rendezvous.

21. Two of His Majesty's Proclamations for prohibiting His Majesty's Subjects from Trading to the East Indies contrary to the Liberties and Privileges granted to the English East India Company, and from being unlawfully concerned in any Foreign Company or Society trading to the East Indies, are enclosed in your Packet one of which must be fixed up in the most convenient part of the Ship for the Perusal of all the Ship's Company.

22. We have permitted your Owners to send out to the Value of Fifty Pounds in Trading Guns Shot and Flints for the purchase of Refreshments at Madagascar if you shall be under the necessity of touching there, but it is on this Condition that in case you do not touch there that the same be delivered at Prime Cost to our President and Council at Fort St. George, and it is our positive directions that on no pretence whatsoever You do dispose of them in any other manner.

23. As it may be necessary for you to touch at some safe and convenient Port in your outward bound Voyage to fill up Your Water and Refresh the People on board Your Ship, You are therefore hereby permitted (notwithstanding any thing in the beforegoing instructions to the contrary) to call in at St. Jaga one of [.................] Islands, where you are to lay in such a stock of Fresh Provisions and Water as will be sufficient to serve you [...........................].

24. A Detachment from His Majestys Royal Regiment of Artillery being to proceed to the East Indies in your Ship you hereby Ordered to afford both the Officers and Private Men all suitable Accommodations, and observe such a Conduct towards them, that there may be no occasions given for discontent and as We have given it in Charge to our Servants abroad to make a particular Enquiry into your behaviour on this Head, you may be assured We shall highly resent any ill usage they may meet with on board your Ship.

25. If the President and Council of Fort St. George or our Select Committee at that Place shall think it for the Interest of the Company to detain you for any particular purposes or send you to any other Ports or Places than are mentioned in these Instructions or the Charterparty, You are to follow all such Orders as they shall give you accordingly and they are to make or cause to be made a reasonable allowance to Your Orders as nearly adequate to the Detention or Service performed as possible.

WE ARE,
YOUR LOVING FRIENDS

LONDON 26th. MARCH 1755.

W. WELLY.
ROBt. JONES.
STEPHEN LARE.
JOHN BOYD.
WILLm. BOWELL.
CHA. CUTTS.
K. COAL BOUGON.
CHAs. YOUTH.

R. DRAKE.
RICHd. CHAUNCY.
W. MABBOTT.
M. IMPEY.
N. NEWNHAM. JUNe.
JOHN PAYNE.
WHICHOTT TURNER,
THOs. PHIPPS.

Appendix VI

Objects found by the survivors on Bird Island:
    Escritoire containing gun flints, a file, wax candles
    Barrels of water, gunpowder, brandy, flour, beer, cider, butter, salt, port, pitch and vinegar
    Pieces of salt pork
    Seven live hogs
    Small boat
    Canvas and cordage
    Bellows
    Company's packets
    Hamper containing gimlets, files, and small needles
    Azimuth compass card, mariner's compass, quadrants
    Ship's scraper, chisel, three sword blades, adze, grapnel, cables, bower (bow) anchor
    Fowling piece
    Camp kettle
    Copper stewpan

Appendixes

Appendixes I to IV are reprinted with permission from the records of the East India Company, **Public Despatches from England, 1754-55, Records of Fort St. George.**

ROBIN GARTON
Fine Art Dealers and Publishers
9 Lancashire Court, New Bond Street, London, W1
01-493 2820

KENNETH GUICHARD: BRITISH ETCHERS 1850–1940

This fine publication, with three original etchings by Robin Tanner, has 380 illustrations and a considerable quantity of previously unpublished information.

It is the only available comprehensive survey of the British School of Etching, with biographies of some 400 artists. Included is reference material on Muirhead Bone, Edmund Blampied, C. R. W. Nevinson and Joseph Webb.

The Folio volume is quarter bound in leather with buckram boards and gilt top edge.

ISBN 0 906030 00 5 **£50**

RAYMOND LISTER: GREAT IMAGES OF BRITISH PRINTMAKING

A survey of the magnificent achievement of British Printmaking during its heyday in the 1920's, tracing its origins to Blake and Bewick. With 64 illustrations, the book shows for the first time some of the related but varied talents which sought expression through the printed image in this country. The incomparable skill which they brought to this medium is demonstrated in its finest examples.

ISBN 0 906030 01 3 Softbound **£3.75**

HEATHER AND ROBIN TANNER: WILTSHIRE VILLAGE

An eye-witness account in word and image of a rural community, lovingly describing its ways, crafts and characters. The book holds an important place in a succession of documents such as *The Natural History of Selborne, Kilvert's Diary* and more recently *Akenfield*. Amongst these, WILTSHIRE VILLAGE is unique, for the record is illustrated by sixty meticulous drawings, faithful to their subject matter, in Robin Tanner's unmistakable style.

ISBN 0 906030 02 1 Edition limited to 100 copies, buckram and leather with Robin Tanner's etching 'The Meadow Stile.' **£75**
ISBN 0 906030 03 X Hardback **£8.95**

GEOFFREY AND DAVID ALLEN: THE GUNS OF SACRAMENTO

The Portuguese galleon *Sacramento* was one of the great men o' war of the 17th century, a 1,000-ton Leviathan mounting some 60 guns. But it was the massive bronze cannon in her hold, cast in Macao for the defence of Portugal that made her maiden voyage so vital. Weighed down with this cargo, a freak storm drove her on to the rocks off Port Elizabeth, where she broke up.

David Allen traced and salvaged the *Sacramento,* bringing 40 bronze cannon ashore in spite of considerable difficulties. Research has brought to light the astonishing account of the surviving crew members who trekked 1,000 miles up the hostile African coast to safety.

ISBN 0 906030 06 4 Hardback **£7.50**

MARTIN MUNCASTER: THE WIND IN THE OAK
The Life, Work and Philosophy of Claude Muncaster. Foreword by H.R.H. Prince Philip.

An affectionate and vivid biography of the prolific and greatly respected painter of dramatic sea-scapes, pastoral landscapes and industrial scenes by his son, the well-known broadcaster. Extracts from his diaries document a varied life. He writes with equal clarity and perception of the gruelling passage in the sailing ship *Olivebank* and the calm, meticulous proceedings at Balmoral and Sandringham where he stayed. He went on to execute some of the most prestigious commissions offered in the post-war years, both by the Royal Family and famous industrialists. The scale of some of the subjects was so vast that painting from a helicopter was the only solution.

ISBN 0 906030 05 6 Hardback **£8.95**